SOUTHERN LIVING COOKBOOK

A Journey Through The Authentic Flavors Of The Past.

Discover All The Recipes And Be Surprised

To See What An Amazing Cook You Are

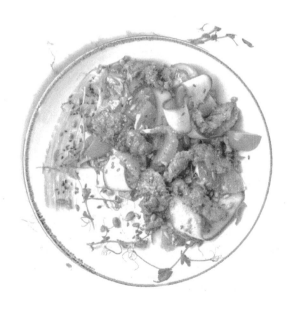

Matt Black

D1133706

2

3

4

INTRODUCTION

Nothing soothes your soul like a plate of Southern cuisine. Southern food sticks to your ribs, whether it's piled high with fried green tomatoes, chicken casserole, potato salad, biscuits, corn bread, or something else entirely. Southern cuisine makes the most of the ingredients available and stretches them without appearing stingy. Southern cooking will always be a part of you if you were born in the South. When my friends leave our hometown, they miss things like sweet tea and good barbecue the most. Whether you grew up with it, married into it, or simply enjoy it, Southern food is a breed all its own. Southern cuisine is edible history, and once you've got sweet tea coursing through your veins, there's no turning back.

Come explore the delights of simple cooking. The emphasis of this book is on Southern cooking. Even though the recipes are simple, the flavors of the dishes are quite amazing.

Southern American cuisine has evolved in America's historically established South. Tidewater, Appalachian, Cajun, Creole, lowland, and Florida cuisines are examples of southern cuisine. Elements of southern cuisine have recently spread north, influencing the production of other types of American cuisine.

Many elements of Southern cooking have been influenced by Southeast American Indian tribes such as the Caddo, Choctaw, and Seminole, including squash, corn (and its derivatives, including grits), and deep-pit barbecuing.

The Southern love of a full breakfast is derived from the British full or fry-up breakfast. Many Appalachian foods are Scottish or Border meals adapted to the current subtropical climate, and pork, once considered informally taboo in Scotland, is used to replace lamb and moth, whereby Southerners eat grit rather than chopped oats, while oatmeal is now much more prevalent than it was previously.

However, areas of the South have other cuisines. Creole cuisine is primarily vernacular in French, West African, and Spanish; other cuisine with noticeable Caribbean influences in Spanish and Tex-Mex has significant influences in the Mexican and Native Americas. In this book, I will share our tried-and-true heirloom recipes along with some lightened-up, healthier versions.

History Of Southern Cooking

All foods are created by combining the tastes and traditions of its populations with ingredients available in the area. Africa, Spain, France, and Scotland all contributed to the evolution of Southern cuisine as we know it today. Each region brought its own ingredients and cooking methods to the table, which were combined with the fresh local foods that are so important to the cuisine. Corn, rice, and nuts, as well as the region's diverse and plentiful seafood and shellfish, all became staples in the people's diets. Okra, watermelon, and sweet potatoes were brought by the Africans. Europeans brought pigs, some of which escaped and became the region's wild hogs. The natives also taught people how to eat local foods such as berries.

During the days of slavery, limiting access to the amount and type of food was used to control the slaves. Their diets were primarily comprised of low-cost foods such as corn and pork, as well as poor or leftover cuts of other meat, which they supplemented by growing some of their own crops at home, such as okra, peanuts, and sweet potato. After their work on the plantation was completed, they tended to these gardens. Some also fished and hunted for possums, rabbits, and squirrels, and they used local ingredients. They made do with what they had, and "soul food" began to emerge.

Preservation techniques also played a role. Africans had little knowledge of meat preservation because their diets were primarily comprised of vegetables and fresh foods. When they were enslaved, however, they had to make every bite count. They learned how to make jerky from the natives, and they also started frying food.

You might be surprised to learn that frying food did not originate in the southern United States or Africa. Animals from hot climates do not need fat reserves to stay warm. Frying was a popular cooking method in Northern Europe and North America. Originally, it was a method of preserving meat. As a result, the colder regions of the south produce more fried food, while the deep south produces more smoking, spicing, and pickling.

Food became a way for people to connect with one another and be comforted. Southerners' souls have been fed by food. It is a way to celebrate life and keep family traditions alive.

With this in mind, we've put together a fantastic collection of the best Soulful Southern recipes. Join us on a journey through some of the best southern food flavors. And now, without further ado, let's get started.

The southern part of America is home to several states that are well-known for their agricultural production. In states such as Louisiana, Georgia, Maryland, Delaware, Ohio, Florida, and North/South Carolina, corn, potatoes, vegetables, nuts, grains, and fruits are widely grown. Furthermore, the vast bodies of water surrounding the coastal areas supplied the region with massive quantities of shrimp, fish, crabs, oysters, and other seafood.

Furthermore, the prosperous lands of the South were home to a variety of game meats such as ducks, deer, birds, and rabbits. Following that, foreign settlers increased the area's meat supply by bringing in pigs and other animals. This sparked the South's love of pork, paving the way for dishes like ham and bacon.

Because of the abundant food supply, both locals and foreigners made southern America their home. The Scotts, Germans, Irish, Spaniards, Africans, French, Mexicans, and Native Americans were among the early settlers who had a significant impact on southern culture and cuisine.

The region's cultural diversity has produced several cuisine types that differ in flavor profile, ingredients and methods. The terms Creole, Cajun, Tex-Mex, Low country and Appalachian are the sub-categories of southern cuisine, with each type armed with a collection of hearty, delicious entrées that provide people with a feeling of warmth, comfort and satisfaction.

Traditional Southern Ingredients

To name a few favorites, we are all familiar with "southern" foods such as fried chicken, jambalaya, collard greens, biscuits, and pecan pie. What many of us don't pause to consider is the complex and unique origins of Southern cuisine.

Chicken

Fried chicken is one of the best-known exports in the region. It is estimated that unlike their English counterparts who baked or boiled chicken, the Scots and later Scottish immigrants to many southern states had a tradition of deep-frying chicken in fat. However there are origins from which Fried Chicken originated in southern and west England, from where most Early settlers came to the south. They conclude that the tradition of sweet meat in southern and western England is solid, as opposed to East Anglia, which favors baking and boiling.

Pork and ham

Pork is used in the kitchen. Southern Marylanders eat stuffed ham. A "pig pickin" is a traditional holiday in Virginia and the Carolinas that includes a whole hog barbecue. Green beans are frequently flavored with bacon and salt pork; turnip greens are stewed with pork and served with vinegar; ham cookies are frequently served with breakfast (biscuits half cut with slices of salt ham served between half of them and red-eyed ham is a popular meal dish). Country ham, a highly salted ham, is popular in the south, with Virginia's Smithfield ham being the most well-known.

Vegetables

Southern cuisine frequently consists of vegetables served with a small amount of meat (especially salt pork). "Beans and greens," white or brown beans served in many parts of the South, with a "mess" of greens stewed in bacon. (Turnip greens are the typical grasses for a meal like this, cooked with a dizzy turbo and a piece of fat.) Beans and maize, with pinto beans stewed with ham or bacon, and John Hoppin's are two other low-calorie southern meals (black-eyed peas, rice, onions, red or green pepper, and bacon).

The cold is primarily used as the foundation for coleslaw, which is served as a side dish as well as on a variety of grilled and fried meats. In southern German-influenced areas such as central Texas, sauteed, vinegar, and sugar-flavored red chocolate is popular.

Butternut squash is popular in the winter and is frequently prepared as a roasted casserole with butter and sweet honey. Green collards and congealed salads are two other traditional vegetable sides. Double stuffed potatoes with bacon, cheddar cheese, cream cheese, mayonnaise, and chives are served in barbeque restaurants across the South.

Rice Country Captain is a regional rice and curry chicken dish that dates back to the 1920s. It became famous after a Columbus, Georgia cook served it to then-President Franklin D. Roosevelt. "This train me

13

with a bucket if you can't give me a party and have Country Captain," George Patton once said.

Seafood

Gulf meats such as black grouper, shrimp, and swordfish can be found in the Mississippi Delta region, while "channel catfish" (Ictalurus punctatus) farmed locally are especially common in Oxford, Mississippi. Local restaurants serve fried catfish pounded in cornmeal with hot sauce and fries and coleslaw on the side. Oysters Rockefeller is a New Orleans specialty that is said to have originated in the city. Creole dishes like jambalayas and gumbo include crawfish, oysters, blue crab, and shrimp.

Buttermilk: This pantry staple can be kept in the back of your fridge for weeks and is essential for fried chicken, biscuits, and pancakes. In a pinch, you can make buttermilk with 1 cup of milk and 1 tablespoon of vinegar or freshly squeezed lemon juice. Using high-fat buttermilk, which can be found at small, local dairies, will add a rich, creamy flavor to baked goods. If you have any leftover buttermilk, freeze it in ice cube trays and store the cubes in a plastic freezer bag, or freeze it in 1-cup containers. Because frozen buttermilk is not as creamy as fresh buttermilk, it is best used for baking after it has been thawed.

Cooking oil: There are numerous options, but the most common are vegetable oil, canola oil, peanut oil, and olive oil.

Peanut oil and vegetable oil have the mildest flavors, but once opened, peanut oil should be stored in a cool, dark place for no more than 4 months. A bottle of extra-virgin olive oil is useful for marinades, drizzling, and preparing salad dressings. Furthermore, solid coconut oil stored at room temperature can be substituted for butter in baked goods.

Cornmeal: Whether you're making corn bread or polenta, cornmeal is a must-have ingredient. There are several types of coarse-ground coffee available, including medium-ground, fine-ground, and stone-ground. Cornmeal that has been finely ground is ideal for batters and corncakes. A thick, dense corn bread is frequently made with medium-ground cornmeal. Use fine-ground cornmeal for a milder corn bread. Stone-ground cornmeal is produced using traditional methods to enhance flavor, but it goes rancid more quickly. It can be kept in the refrigerator for up to 4 months in an airtight container.

Grits: What's the difference between grits and cornmeal anyway? Grits and cornmeal are both made from corn but are a world apart. Grits are usually made from ground hominy treated with lye. It makes for a creamier consistency when cooked. There are several types of grits: quick cooking, ready in five minutes or less; instant, which comes in packets; and stone-ground grits, which are slower to cook and are the ones usually found in recipes. Stone-ground grits can be stored in an airtight container in the pantry for up to 1 year, or indefinitely in the freezer.

Flour: This is a must for baking, thickening, or making gravy. All-purpose flour can be stored in an airtight container in the refrigerator or in a cool, dry place in the pantry for up to 2 years, or indefinitely in the freezer. If a recipe calls for self-rising flour, make your own by adding 1½ teaspoons baking powder and ½ teaspoon salt to 1 cup of all-purpose flour.

Spices and Seasonings: These add flavor to dishes without adding extra calories. A basic spice cabinet should include:

Black pepper (if possible, get a spice mill and grind your own fresh)

Cayenne pepper

Chili powder

Italian seasoning

Salt (preferably sea salt)

Other ingredients you'll want to have available for baking include:

Baking powder

Baking soda

Ground cinnamon

Vanilla extract (You can make your own: Add 1 vanilla bean to a pint of vodka and store it in a cool, dark place for 1 month before using.)

Sugar: Whether you're baking or making the perfect glass of sweet tea, it's a good idea to keep all three types of sugar on hand: brown, granulated, and confectioners'. Each will last indefinitely if stored in an airtight container in a cool, dry place. Sugar can also be frozen in an airtight container indefinitely. Brown sugar, on the other hand, will become as hard as a brick if not stored properly. To break up the lumps, simply place it in a blender or food processor and process for 10 seconds.

Eggs: Eggs are used for a variety of purposes, including baking and breakfast. These inexpensive fridge additions can also be used for dinner in a pinch. Who can say no to an omelet? Simply fill with leftover meat, onions, peppers, and cheese. Hard-boiled eggs can be used to make egg salad or the Southern favorite, deviled eggs. Eggs can be frozen by breaking them, lightly beating them, and pouring them into ice cube trays. Freeze until completely solid. Place the frozen cubes in freezer-safe containers. Once thawed, the eggs can be stored for up to a year and used for baking.

Milk is a must-have in the refrigerator because it is used in sauces, baking, and so much more. Whole milk is used in many recipes that call for "milk." When skim milk is used in a recipe, the fat content changes, making the end result drier. Having said that, I keep 2% milk on hand unless I'm making a special dessert or sauce that I know will benefit from the flavor. If you don't use milk often, buy a box of powdered milk for baking. It can be stored in the pantry and mixed as needed with 3 tablespoons of dried milk to 1 cup of water.

To accommodate allergies or preferences, nut or soy milks can be substituted. It's something we do on a regular basis at our house.

Pasta: This pantry staple can keep for months on the shelf. It's good to have on hand for a quick meal, but it can also be used in soups or stews, pasta salads, and as the basis of casseroles and skillet meals. When adding to soup or skillet meals, wait until the dish is nearly done, and then add the pasta and simmer until the noodles are cooked but still firm. Adding noodles too early soaks up the moisture and results in a drier dish and soggy noodles.

Enjoy cooking!

CHAPTER 1: MAIN DISHES

Fried Green Tomato

Preparation Time: 10 Minutes

Cooking Time: 10 Minutes

Servings: 3

Ingredients:

kosher salt

freshly ground pepper

4 medium green tomatoes, cut into ½ inch slices (discard ends)

¼ cup corn oil, plus more if needed

2/3 cup corn meal

1/3 cup white flour

1 egg (or 2 egg whites), beaten

DIRECTIONS:

Salt and pepper tomato slices

Heat oil to medium-hot in a large non-stick skillet.

Combine corn meal and flour.

Dip tomato slices in egg and dredge in corn meal mixture.

Fry tomato slices in oil until golden brown, approximately 4-5 minutes on each side.

Add more oil to pan if needed.

If oil becomes too hot, it will smoke and tomatoes may burn.

Drain tomatoes on paper towels and serve immediately.

Nutrition: calories 121, fat 3, fiber 6, carbs 14, protein 6

Louisiana Red Bean and Rice

Preparation Time: 10 Minutes

Cooking Time: 25 Minutes

Servings: 3

Ingredients

1 pound andouille sausage, sliced

1 pound kidney beans

¼ cup olive oil

1 large onion, chopped

1 green bell pepper, chopped

2 celery stalks, chopped

2 tablespoons garlic, minced

½ teaspoon cayenne pepper

1 tablespoon dried parsley

¼ teaspoon dried sage

1 teaspoon dried thyme

1 teaspoon Cajun seasoning

2 cups long grain white rice

4 cups beef broth

6 cups water

2 bay leaves

DIRECTIONS:

Soak the beans in water in a large saucepan overnight.

In a medium sized skillet, heat the oil over medium heat, and sauté onion, celery, bell pepper, and garlic in olive oil for 3 to 4 minutes

Rinse the beans and cover them with 6 cups of water.

Add cooked vegetables to the beans, and stir in the cayenne pepper, parsley, sage, thyme, bay leaves, and Cajun seasoning.

Bring the mixture to a boil, and reduce the heat to medium low, and simmer for 2 ½ hours.

Stir the sausage into the beans and allow it to simmer for 30 minutes.

In a saucepan, boil 4 cups beef broth, and add the rice. Reduce the heat, cover it and allow it to simmer for 20 minutes. You can also use a rice cooker.

Serve the bean mixture over the hot rice.

Nutrition: calories 167, fat 4, fiber 7, carbs 15, protein 6

Old-Country Pork Meatballs

Preparation Time: 10 Minutes

Cooking Time: 40 Minutes

Servings: 3

Ingredients:

1 pound ground pork

½ cup dried bread crumbs

4 large eggs

½ cup whole milk

6 ounces Parmesan, freshly grated

¼ cup sweet onion, minced

2 cloves garlic, minced

2 tablespoons fresh parsley, finely chopped

2 tablespoons fresh basil, finely chopped

DIRECTIONS:

Preheat the oven to 350°F, and prepare a baking sheet with aluminum foil and cooking spray.

In a large mixing bowl, combine all the ingredients together, adding more breadcrumbs if the mixture seems too wet.

Roll the meatballs out to the size of golf balls, and arrange them on the baking sheet. Bake for 35 to 40 minutes, or until they are no longer pink in the center.

Nutrition: Calories: 221Kcal Carbohydrates: 4.2g Proteins: 10.8g Fat: 15.4g

Southern Smothered Pork

Preparation Time: 10 Minutes

Cooking Time: 25 Minutes

Servings: 3

Ingredients:

1 (3 pound) boneless pork loin roast

1 tablespoon Creole seasoning

1 teaspoon salt

½ teaspoon freshly ground black pepper

6 ounces thick cut bacon, diced

⅓ cup all-purpose flour

1 large yellow onion, finely chopped

1 rib celery, finely chopped

½ medium green bell pepper, seeded and chopped

24

1 tablespoon garlic, minced

6 ounces button mushrooms, thinly sliced

4 cups canned low-sodium beef broth

1 tablespoon Worcestershire sauce

2 tablespoons sliced green onion tops

Cooked white rice, for serving

DIRECTIONS:

Season the roast evenly with Creole seasoning, salt, and black pepper, and with clean hands, rub it into the meat.

Heat a Dutch oven and cook the bacon until it is crispy, about 6 minutes. Using a slotted spoon, transfer the bacon to paper towels to drain, and set it aside.

Place the roast in the bacon grease in the skillet, and increase the heat to high. Cook until the roast is evenly browned on all sides, about 8-10 minutes. Remove the roast to a plate and cover it loosely with foil.

Add the flour to the drippings in the pan and cook, stirring constantly, until a roux the color of milk chocolate is formed, 1-2 minutes. You can add a little butter if the mixture becomes too thick. Add the chopped onion, celery, bell pepper, and cook, stirring, until the vegetables have wilted, about 5 minutes. Stir in the beef broth and Worcestershire sauce.

Reduce the heat to low, and place the roast back in the pan. Turn to coat it in the gravy. Cover the pan and cook over low heat, turning occasionally, until an instant-read thermometer inserted into the center of the roast registers 145-150°F, about 45 minutes longer.

Remove the roast from the pan and transfer to a platter. Add the green onion tops to the sauce and cook for 10 to 15 minutes, uncovered, until the sauce is thick enough to coat the back of a spoon. Stir the reserved crispy bacon into the sauce, slice the roast and serve, with the sauce ladled over the roast and cooked white rice alongside.

Nutrition: Calories: 205Kcal Carbohydrates: 4.4g Proteins: 8g Fat: 17.2g

Traditional Meat Pie

Preparation Time: 10 Minutes

Cooking Time: 35 Minutes

Servings: 3

Ingredients

1 pound ground pork

1 pound ground beef

2 celery stalks, finely diced

1 green bell pepper, chopped

1 large baking potato, peeled and finely chopped

1 bay leaf

1 teaspoon dried thyme leaves

3 cloves of garlic, minced

1 small carrot

1 large onion

1 cup hot water

1 teaspoon Worcestershire sauce

2 beef bouillon cubes

2 tablespoons chopped fresh parsley

Salt free seasoning blend to taste

Salt and pepper to taste

1 egg, separated

2 tablespoons of water

2 sheets frozen puff pastry

2 cups shredded cheddar cheese

Cooking spray

DIRECTIONS:

Preheat the oven to 350°F, and coat a 9x13 inch dish with cooking spray.

Put a large nonstick skillet over medium high heat and mix the ground pork and beef, cooking until brown and crumbly, about 6-8 minutes. Discard the excess grease.

Add the bell pepper, celery, onions and stir, then cover the pan and reduce the heat to medium.

Stir frequently, until the vegetables have softened and the onions are translucent, about 4-6 minutes.

Make a well in the center of the skillet; place the garlic on the bottom of the pan for a few seconds, and then blend with the meat.

Add the parsley, carrot, bay leaf, thyme, potato, Worcestershire sauce, seasoning blend, and salt and pepper to taste.

In a bowl, dissolve the bouillon cubes in hot water then pour it into the meat mixture and mix it well. Bring to a boil then reduce the heat from medium to low. Cover and simmer for 10 to 15 minutes until the carrots have softened.

In the prepared baking dish, lay one sheet of puff pastry. Gently push the pastry into the corners of the baking dish. Gently spoon the meat mixture into the crust and spread evenly. Avoid adding liquid to the pie as it will cause it to become soggy. Top the mixture with cheddar cheese.

In a small bowl, whisk together the egg yolk and a tablespoon of water.

Brush the edges of the bottom of the puff pastry sheet.

Lay the second sheet of puff pastry on the top and seal the edges by pressing with a fork.

Mix the egg white with remaining tablespoon of water, and brush the top surface of the pastry. Poke holes with a fork to vent the crust.

Preheat the oven to 350°F and bake the pie until the pastry has turned golden brown. Keep checking your pie after every 15 minutes to prevent your pie from over burning. Serve hot.

Nutrition: Calories: 294Kcal Carbohydrates: 3g Proteins: 14g Fat: 24g

Shrimp and Grits

Preparation Time: 10 Minutes

Cooking Time: 20 Minutes

Servings: 3

Ingredients

1 ½ pounds peeled and deveined shrimp

½ teaspoon hot sauce

3 tablespoons fresh lemon juice

2 bacon slices, chopped

½ cup chopped green onions, plus a few tablespoons for serving

1 ½ cup green bell pepper, chopped

1 cup chicken broth

5 cups water

1 tablespoon butter

1 teaspoon salt

1 ½ cups chopped grits

1 ½ teaspoons minced garlic

¾ cup shredded cheddar cheese

DIRECTIONS:

In a medium sized bowl, combine the shrimp, hot sauce, and lemon juice.

Cook bacon in a skillet over medium heat until nice and crisp.

Add ½ cup green onions, bell pepper and garlic to the pan and allow it to cook for 5 minutes until tender, stirring occasionally.

Stir in the broth, shrimp mixture, and ¼ cup of green onions, and allow the mixture to cook for 5 minutes, until the shrimp have completely cooked.

In another saucepan, bring the water to a boil and then stir in the grits.

Lower the heat to low and allow it to simmer, covered, for 5 minutes until the mixture has thickened.

Stir in butter and add salt to taste.

Serve the shrimp over the grits, with shredded cheese and green onion sprinkled on top.

Nutrition:

Calories: 141 Cal

Carbs: 2 g

Fat: 10 g

Protein: 8 g

Fiber: 0 g

Beer Battered and Fried Pickles

Preparation Time: 10 Minutes

Cooking Time: 35 Minutes

Servings: 3

Ingredients for Your Fried Pickles:

2 Jars of Dill Pickles, Sandwich Sliced and Drained

1 Eggs, Large in Size and Beaten

1 Can of Beer, Dark and Your Favorite Kind

1 teaspoon of Salt, For Taste

1 ½ Cups of Flour, All Purpose Variety

Some Vegetable Oil

Ingredients for Your Spicy Ranch Dipping Sauce:

¾ Cup of Buttermilk

½ Cup of Mayonnaise, Your Favorite Kind

2 Tablespoons of Green Onions, Minced

1 Clove of Garlic, Minced

1 teaspoon of Hot Sauce, Your Favorite Kind

½ teaspoons of Salt, For Taste

Some Salt for Garnish

DIRECTIONS:

1. First prepare your pickles. To do this first dry your pickles with some paper towels.

2. Then whisk together your egg and next 3 ingredients together in a large sized bowl. Add in your flour and continue whisking until smooth in consistency.

3. Then pout a generous amount of oil in a large sized skillet over medium to high heat. Once the oil is hot enough dip your slices into your batter and hold to allow the excess to drip off. Place your batter covered pickles into your oil and cook until golden in color. Drain on a plate lined with paper towels. Allow to cool slightly.

4. Then prepare your dipping sauce. To do this whisk together your first 6 Ingredients for your dipping sauce until smooth in consistency. Then garnish with some extra salt. Serve alongside your fried pickles and enjoy.

Nutrition: Calories 128 Fat 6.2 g, Carbohydrates 16.3 g, Sugar 3.3 g, Protein 3.2 g, Cholesterol 17 mg

Tasty Fried Okra with Pecans

Preparation Time: 10 Minutes

Cooking Time: 35 Minutes

Servings: 3

List of Ingredients:

1 Cup of Pecans, Crushed

1 ½ Cups of Baking Mix, All Purpose Variety

1 teaspoon of Salt, For Taste

½ teaspoons of Pepper, For Taste

2 Packs of Okra, Whole, Frozen and thawed

Some Peanut Oil, For Frying

DIRECTIONS:

1. First place your pecans in a very thin layer inside of a shallow baking pan.

2. Bake your pecans for the next 10 minutes or until lightly toasted. Make sure that you stir it occasionally.

3. Then add in your lightly toasted pecans and next 3 ingredients into a food processor. Blend on the highest setting or until fine in consistency. Pour mixture into a large sized bowl.

4. Add your thawed okra to this mixture and toss gently to coat.

5. Next add your peanut oil into a large sized skillet and heat over medium to high heat. Once the oil is hot enough add in your okra and fry for the next 6 minutes or until golden in color. Drain on a plate lined with paper towels. Serve whenever you are ready.

Nutrition: Calories: 340 Fat: 15g Carbohydrates: 32g Protein: 15g Sugar: 0g Cholesterol: 0mg

Southern Style Collard Greens

Preparation Time: 10 Minutes

Cooking Time: 25 Minutes

Servings: 3

List of Ingredients:

12 Bacon Slices, Hickory Smoked and Chopped Finely

2 Onions, Sweet Flavored, Medium in Size and Chopped Finely

¾ Pounds of Ham, Smoked Variety and Chopped Finely

6 Cloves of Garlic, Finely Chopped

3 Contains of Chicken Broth, Homemade Preferable

3 Packs of Collard Greens, Fresh

1/3 Cup of Vinegar, Apple Cider Variety

1 tablespoon of Sugar, White

1 teaspoon of Salt, For Taste

¾ teaspoons of Pepper, For Taste

DIRECTIONS:

1. The first thing that you will want to do is cook your bacon in a large sized skillet set to medium to high heat for the next 10 to 12 minutes or until crispy to the touch.

2. Then add in your onion and continue to cook for the next 8 minutes.

3. After this time add in your chopped garlic and smoked ham. Cook for an addition minute then add in your remaining ingredients. Mix together until evenly mixed.

4. Dump your contents into a slow cooker and cook on the lowest setting for the next 2 hours or done to your desired doneness. After this time serve whenever you are ready and enjoy.

Nutrition: Calories: 90 Cal Carbs: 0.6 g Fat: 7 g Protein: 6.3 g Fiber: 0 g

Shrimp Balls

Preparation Time: 10 Minutes

Cooking Time: 25 Minutes

Servings: 3

Ingredients:

1½ pounds (675 g) small shrimps, shelled, cleaned, and roughly chopped

The tomato broth

⅛ teaspoon coriander seeds

⅓ cup (85 ml) finely chopped white onion

1 cup (250 ml) nopales, cooked

1 cup (250 ml) peeled, diced potatoes (about 6 ounces/180 g)

1½ cups (375 ml) peeled and diced chayote (approximately eight ounces/225 g)

1½ pounds (675 g) tomatoes, finely chopped (approximately four cups/1 l)

2 teaspoons salt, or to taste

3 garlic cloves, finely chopped

3 tablespoons vegetable oil

4 cups (1 l) water

5 peppercorns

Shrimp ball seasoning

¼ teaspoon coriander seeds

¼ teaspoon peppercorns

½ ancho chile, veins and seeds removed

½-inch (1.5-cm) piece of cinnamon stick, broken up

1 tablespoon vegetable oil

1½ garlic cloves

1½ teaspoons salt, or to taste

3 tablespoons water

DIRECTIONS:

Place the shrimps into the freezer for approximately 2 hours, until they are slightly frozen (this will make it easier to grind them in the blender or food processor).

In the meantime, prepare the tomato broth. In a wide, heavy pan, heat the oil and fry the tomatoes, onion, and garlic, stirring them occasionally and scraping the bottom of the pan, until they are reduced to a thick sauce. Put in the 4 cups (1 l) of water, salt, peppercorns, and coriander seeds and bring to its boiling point. Put in the potatoes and cook for approximately ten minutes, then put in the chayote and cook until nearly soft, approximately fifteen minutes more. Put in the nopales and just heat through. Tweak the seasoning.

Prepare the seasoning for the shrimp balls by first soaking the ancho chile in hot water for fifteen minutes, then drain and put in a blender jar. Crush the coriander seeds, peppercorns, and cinnamon stick. Put in the spices to the blender jar, together with the salt, garlic, and water, and blend to a paste. Heat the oil and fry the seasoning paste using high heat for approximately 2 minutes. Set aside.

Combine the slightly frozen shrimps to a quite smooth consistency. Put in the fried seasoning and work it in well with your hands. Lightly grease your hands, then make the mixture into balls approximately 1¼ inches (3.5 cm) in diameter—there must be 18 of them. Cautiously place the shrimp balls into the simmering broth, then cover the pan and continue simmering for approximately fifteen minutes, turning them once during the cooking time.

Serve the shrimp balls in deep soup bowls, with sufficient the broth and vegetables.

Nutrition: Calories: 129 Cal, Carbs: 2 g, Fat: 8 g, Protein: 11 g, Fiber: 1.4 g.

Chicken With Grapes

Preparation Time: 10 Minutes

Cooking Time: 30 Minutes

Servings: 3

Ingredients:

⅔ cup (165 ml) dry white wine

1 cup (250 ml) thinly cut white onion

1 pound (450 g) seedless white grapes

2 big chickens, approximately 3 pounds (1.35 kg) each

2 celery ribs, chopped

2 garlic cloves

2 pounds (900 g) tomatoes, roughly chopped (about 4¼ cups/1.65 l)

2 tablespoons butter

2 tablespoons vegetable oil

6 sprigs fresh marjoram or ½ teaspoon dried

6 sprigs fresh thyme or ½ teaspoon dried

Salt and freshly ground pepper

DIRECTIONS:

Preheat your oven to 350° f (180° c).

Truss the chickens. Heat the butter and oil together in a deep flameproof casserole and brown the chickens well all over. Flavour them with salt and pepper, remove, and set them aside.

In the same fat, fry the onion, garlic, and celery using low heat for approximately five minutes. Put in the tomatoes and herbs to the pan.

Put the chickens on their sides in the tomato mixture. Cover the pan and bake for approximately twenty minutes.

Turn the chickens over and carry on baking them until they become soft—twenty to twenty-five minutes. Turn off the oven. Move them to a warmed serving dish and return to a warm oven.

Combine the vegetables and juices in the pan to a smooth sauce. Return to the pan and cook it on moderate heat until it has reduced and thickened—about ten minutes. Put in the wine and carry on cooking the sauce for approximately 3 minutes, stirring it occasionally. Put in the grapes and carry on cooking the sauce over brisk heat for about three minutes more.

Nutrition: Calories 113 Total Carbs 12g Net Carbs 6g Protein 1g Fat 7g Sugar 3g Fiber 6g

Chicken With Pumpkin Seed Sauce

Preparation Time: 10 Minutes

Cooking Time: 35 Minutes

Servings: 3

Ingredients:

¼ cup sesame seeds

⅓ cup pepitas

1 cup fresh cilantro leaves

1 jalapeño chile, stemmed, seeded, and chopped

1 onion, chopped fine

1 tablespoon lime juice

1 teaspoon fresh minced thyme or ¼ teaspoon dried

1½ cups chicken broth

2 tablespoons vegetable oil

3 garlic cloves, minced

4 (6 to 8 ounce) boneless, skinless chicken breasts, trimmed

6 ounces fresh tomatillos, husks and stems removed, washed well and dried, chopped

Pinch sugar

Salt and pepper

DIRECTIONS:

Toast pepitas and sesame seeds in 12 inch nonstick frying pan on moderate heat until seeds are golden and aromatic, approximately fifteen minutes; move to container. Reserve 1 tablespoon toasted seeds separately for decoration.

Put in oil, onion, and ½ teaspoon salt to now empty frying pan and cook over moderate high heat until tender, five to seven minutes. Mix in jalapeño, garlic, and thyme and cook until aromatic, approximately half a minute. Mix in tomatillos, broth, and toasted seeds, cover, and cook until tomatillos start to tenderize, approximately ten minutes.

Sprinkle the chicken with salt and pepper, then nestle into frying pan. Cover, decrease the heat to moderate low, and cook until chicken records 160 degrees, ten to fifteen minutes, turning midway through cooking. Move chicken to platter, tent with aluminium foil, and allow to rest for five to ten minutes.

Cautiously move mixture left in frying pan to blender. Put in cilantro, lime juice, and sugar and pulse until mostly smooth, approximately one minute. Sprinkle with salt and pepper to taste. Ladle some of sauce over chicken and drizzle with reserved seeds. Serve with rest of the sauce.

Nutrition: Calories 176 Total Carbs 5g Net Carbs 2g Protein 8g Fat 15g Sugar 1g Fiber 3g

Summer Squash Casserole

Preparation Time: 10 Minutes

Cooking Time: 50 Minutes

Servings: 3

Ingredients

2 pounds yellow summer squash

1 large onion, chopped

7 tablespoons butter, divided

1 large clove garlic, chopped

½ green bell pepper, chopped

½ red bell pepper, chopped

4 slices plain white bread, toasted

1 jalapeño pepper, seeded and chopped

24 round buttery crackers, crumbled in a food processor

½ cup heavy whipping cream

½ pound sharp cheddar cheese

1 teaspoon salt

1 teaspoon sugar

4 large eggs, beaten

¼ teaspoon cayenne pepper

DIRECTIONS:

Heat the oven to 350°F, and grease a 2-quart baking dish with butter.

Cut the squash to ½ inch thick slices, and boil in salted water for 10 minutes, until cooked through.

Drain the squash, and purée in a food processor.

Over medium heat, melt 6 tablespoons of butter, add onion, peppers, and garlic, and cook until the mixture is tender.

In the meantime, put the toasts in a food processor and reduce to crumbs.

Melt the remaining butter and combine it with the crumbs. Set aside.

Combine the squash puree, garlic, crackers, cheese, peppers, and onion in a large bowl, and mix well. Stir in the sugar, cream, egg, and seasonings, and blend.

Pour the mixture into a baking dish.

Top it with toast crumbs, and bake for 40 minutes until browned.

MUSTARD SAUCE (Senfsosse)

Follow recipe for White Sauce, using stock as the liquid. Put in 2 tablespoons sharp German mustard to sauce for last five minutes of cooking time.

Finish with a dab of butter. Serve with fish, asparagus or cauliflower.

TOMATO CREAM SAUCE (Tomaten-Rahmsosse)

Follow recipe for White Sauce, and simmer ten minutes. Put in 1 small can seasoned tomato sauce and simmer fifteen minutes.

Sprinkle with salt, sugar and a dash of lemon juice.

Nutrition: Calories 158 Total Carbs 10g net Carbs 6g Protein 12g Fat 9g Sugar 4g Fiber 4g

Little Pieces Of Browned Pork

Preparation Time: 10 Minutes

Cooking Time: 1 hour

Servings: 3

Ingredients:

2 teaspoons salt, or to taste

3 pounds (1.35 kg) boneless pork shoulder, with fat

DIRECTIONS:

Chop the meat, with the fat, into strips about 2 by ¾ inches (5 by 2 cm). Barely cover the meat with water in a heavy, wide pan. Put in the salt and bring to its boiling point, uncovered. Reduce the heat and allow the meat to carry on cooking briskly until all the liquid has vaporized—by this time it must be thoroughly cooked but not falling apart.

Reduce the heat a little and carry on cooking the meat until all the fat has rendered out of it. Keep turning the meat until it is mildly browned all over—total cooking time is approximately 1 hour and ten minutes.

Serve instantly for best flavor and texture.

Nutrition: Calories: 482 Fat: 23.41 Carbohydrates: 0g Protein: 16.59 Sugar: 0g

Mexican Style Shrimp Cocktail

Preparation Time: 10 Minutes

Cooking Time: 35 Minutes

Servings: 3

Ingredients:

¼ cup chopped fresh cilantro, stems reserved

½ cup ketchup

1 avocado, halved, pitted, and slice into ½ inch pieces

1 cucumber, peeled, halved along the length, seeded, and slice into ½ inch pieces

1 small red onion, chopped fine

1 tablespoon hot sauce

1 tablespoon sugar

1 teaspoon black peppercorns

1½ pounds medium shrimp (41 to 50 per pound), peeled, deveined, and tails removed

2 cups Clamato juice

2 tablespoons lime juice, plus lime wedges for serving

3 tomatoes, cored and slice into ½ inch pieces

Salt and pepper

DIRECTIONS:

Mix shrimp, 3 cups water, cilantro stems, peppercorns, sugar, and 1 teaspoon salt in big deep cooking pan. Put deep cooking pan on moderate heat and cook, stirring once in a while, until shrimp are pink and firm to touch, about eight to ten minutes (water must be just bubbling around edge of deep cooking pan and register 165 degrees). Remove deep cooking pan from heat, cover, and let shrimp sit in cooking liquid for a couple of minutes.

In the meantime, fill big container with ice water. Drain shrimp into colander, discarding cilantro stems and spices. Instantly move shrimp to ice water to stop cooking and chill meticulously, approximately 3 minutes. Remove shrimp from ice water and meticulously pat dry using paper towels.

Mix tomatoes, cucumber, onion, Clamato juice, ketchup, lime juice, and hot sauce together in serving container. Mix in shrimp, cover, and place in your fridge for minimum 30 minutes. (Shrimp cocktail can be placed in your fridge for maximum one day; allow it to sit at room temperature for about ten minutes before you serve.) Mix in avocado and chopped cilantro and sprinkle with salt and pepper to taste and serve.

Nutrition: Calories 198, Carbohydrates 16g, Fiber 2g, Cholesterol 231mg, Sugar 1g, Fat 9g, Protein 14g

Bayou Style Fried Shrimp

Preparation Time: 10 Minutes

Cooking Time: 25 Minutes

Servings: 3

List of Ingredients:

3 Pounds of Shrimp, Large in Size, Unpeeled and Raw

2 Cups of Milk, Whole

1 Egg, Large in Size and Beaten

1 tablespoon of Mustard, Yellow in Color

1 teaspoon of Cajun Style Seasoning

1 Pack of Fish Dry Mix, Dry

1 tablespoon of Cajun Style, Seasoning

Some Vegetable Oil

Some Remoulade Sauce

DIRECTIONS:

1. First peel your shrimp, making sure that you leave the tails on the shrimp. Then cut your shrimp butterfly style and devein them. Place into a large sized bowl. Set aside for later use.

2. Whisk together your next 4 ingredients until evenly mixed together. Pour this mixture over your shrimp and allow to stand for the next 15 minutes.

3. Then combine your dry fish fry mix and Cajun style seasoning together. Dredge your shrimp in your fish fry mixture and make sure to shake off the excess. Place onto a generously greased baking sheet.

4. Then pour your oil into a large sized skillet and heat over medium to high heat. Once the oil is hot enough add in your shrimp and fry until golden brown in color. Once fried place on wire racks to drain and serve whenever you are ready.

Nutrition: Calories: 392; Total fat: 4gSaturated fat: 1gProtein: 15gCarbs: 71gSugar: 11gFiber:

Classic Shrimp Po'boys

Preparation Time: 10 Minutes

Cooking Time: 35 Minutes

Servings: 3

Ingredients for Your Po'boys:

2 Pounds of Shrimp, Large in Size, Unpeeled and Fresh

1 ¼ Cups of Flour, All Purpose Variety

½ teaspoons of Salt, For Taste

½ teaspoons of Pepper, For Taste

½ Cup of Milk, Whole

1 Eggs, Large in Size and Beaten

Some Peanut Oil

1/3 Cup of Butter, Soft

1 teaspoon of Garlic, Minced

4 Bread Rolls, French and Split

1 Cup of Lettuce, Shredded

Ingredients for Your Remoulade Sauce:

1 Cup of Mayonnaise, Your Favorite Kind

3 Green Onions, Finely Sliced

2 Tablespoons of Mustard, Creole Variety

1 tablespoon of Parsley, Fresh and Finely Chopped

1 teaspoon of Garlic, Minced

1 teaspoon of Horseradish

DIRECTIONS:

1. The first thing that you will want to do is peel and devein your shrimp.

2. Then combine your next 3 Ingredients for your po'boys in a medium sized bowl. Then stir together your large egg and whole milk together in a small sized bowl or until smooth in consistency.

3. Then toss your shrimp in your milk mixture and dredge in your flour mixture. Shake off the excess and set aside.

4. Next pour your peanut oil in a large sized skillet and heat over medium to high heat. Once hot enough add in your shrimp and fry for the next 2 minutes or until golden in color. Once done drain on some wire racks.

5. Then melt your butter in a medium sized bowl. Once melted add in your garlic. Then take your rolls and spread them evenly in your butter mixture.

6. Place your rolls into your oven to bake at 450 degrees for at least 8 minutes.

7. While your rolls are baking prepare your remoulade sauce. To do this stir together all of your remoulade ingredients together and chill until ready to use.

8. Remove your rolls from your oven and place your shrimp inside of it. Top with lettuce and remoulade sauce and enjoy immediately.

Nutrition: 190 cal.15g fat 7g protein 4g carbs.

Southern Style Rice and Red Beans

Preparation Time: 10 Minutes

Cooking Time: 7 hours

Servings: 3

List of Ingredients:

1 Pound of Red Beans, Dried

7 Cups of Water, Warm

1 Green Bell Pepper, Finely Chopped

1 Onion, Medium in Size and Finely Chopped

1 Onion, Medium in Size and Finely Chopped

3 Stalks of Celery, Finely Chopped

3 Cloves of Garlic, Finely Chopped

½ Pound of Sausage, Andouille Variety and Thinly Sliced

3 Tablespoons of Creole Style Seasoning

Some Rice, Hot and Cooked

Some Green Onions for Garnishing

DIRECTIONS:

1. Place your first 8 ingredients in a small sized slow cooker.

2. Cover and cook on the highest setting for the next 7 hours or until your beans are tender to the touch.

3. After this time remove and serve with some hot rice. Garnish with some sliced green onions and enjoy.

Nutrition:75 cal. 6g fat 8g protein 1g carbs.

Hearty Southern Style Brisket

Preparation Time: 10 Minutes

Cooking Time: 2 hours

Servings: 3

List of Ingredients:

4 Chilies, Guajillo Variety

4 Cups of Water, Boiling

½ Cup of Vinegar, Cider Variety

½ Cup of Chicken Broth, Low in Sodium and Homemade Preferable

8 Cloves of Garlic

1 Onion, Medium in Size and Finely Chopped

3 Sprigs of Thyme, Fresh

2 teaspoons of Oregano Leaves, Mexican Style and Dried

1 ½ tp. Of Cumin, Ground

½ teaspoons of Cloves, Ground

½ teaspoons of Allspice, Ground

3 teaspoons of Salt, For Taste and Evenly Divided

2 teaspoons of Pepper, For Taste

1 Beef Brisket, Flat

8 Cups of Wood Chips, Hickory Style

2 Limes, Large in Size and Cut Into Small Wedges

Some Sprigs of Cilantro, Fresh

DIRECTIONS:

1. The first thing that you will want to do is cook your chilies in a large sized skillet place over high heat for the next 5 minutes or until they are fragrant, making sure to turn them over often. Then place your chilies into a large sized bowl. Add 4 cups of water that is boiling into the bowl and allow to stand for at least 20 minutes. After 20 minutes remove and drain.

2. Then process your drained chilies and the next 9 ingredients into a food processor. Blend on the highest setting or until smooth in consistency.

3. Season your salt and pepper generously over your brisket and place into a shallow dish. Pour this chile mix over your brisket and rub generously all over your brisket. Cover and chill for the next 2 hours to marinate.

4. While your brisket is marinating soak your wood chips for the next 30 minutes. Then preheat your grill to at least 250 to 300 degrees.

5. Place your drained wood chips into a large sized aluminum foil dish and cover with a sheet of aluminum foil. Poke a few holes into the foil and place your chips onto your grill.

6. Then remove your brisket from the marinade and place into a large sized roasting pan. Place pan onto your grill and grill for at least 1 ½ hours or until your brisket is completely cooked. Remove and carve. Enjoy while still warm.

Nutrition:150 cal.9g fat 8g protein 4g carbs.

Chicken With Fried Bread Crumbs

Preparation Time: 10 Minutes

Cooking Time: 35 Minutes

Servings: 3

Ingredients:

¼ cup (65 ml) thinly cut white onion

⅓ cup (85 ml) vegetable oil

½ small white onion

1 chorizo, crumbled and fried

1 pound (450 g) tomatoes, broiled

1½ cups (375 ml) dried but not toasted bread crumbs

2 garlic cloves, thinly cut

2 tablespoons slivered almonds

2 teaspoons juice from the chile can

3 jalapeño chiles en escabeche

3 medium carrots, scraped and slice into ½-inch (1.5-cm) cubes

3 medium zucchini (12 ounces/340 g), cut into ½-inch (1.5-cm) cubes

3 tablespoons raisins

3 tablespoons vegetable oil

5 peppercorns

A 4-pound (1.8-kg) chicken, cut into several pieces

Salt to taste

Water or chicken broth to cover

DIRECTIONS:

Place the chicken into a big pan with the onion, 1 garlic clove, the peppercorns, and salt, cover with cold water, and bring to a simmer. Continue simmering for approximately fifteen minutes, put in the carrots, and cook for ten more minutes. Put in the zucchini and carry on cooking using low heat until the chicken is just soft and the vegetables still a little firm to the bite, approximately ten minutes. Strain, saving for later the stock.

Heat the oil in a flameproof casserole and lightly fry the onion and remaining garlic until translucent.

Combine the tomatoes to a quite smooth sauce and put in to the onion with ½ cup (125 ml) of the reserved stock. Allow the sauce reduce on moderate heat for approximately five minutes.

Put in the chicken pieces and vegetables, the raisins, almonds, chorizo, chiles, and chile juice and cook slowly for eight minutes more, stirring the mixture occasionally to prevent sticking. The sauce by then must be reduced.

Heat the oil in a frying pan, put in the bread crumbs, and fry them, stirring them all the time until they are a uniform gold color, approximately eight minutes. Then drizzle the bread crumbs over the chicken and vegetables and serve instantly.

Nutrition:90 Cal 7 g Fats 5.6 g Protein; 0.7 g Net Carb 0.6 g Fiber

Rice With Shrimp

Preparation Time: 10 Minutes

Cooking Time: 15 Minutes

Servings: 3

Ingredients:

¾ cup (185 ml) finely chopped white onion

1 cup (250 ml) fruity (but not extra virgin) olive oil

1 small red bell pepper, cleaned of veins and seeds, thinly cut

1 teaspoon dried mexican oregano

1½ cups (375 ml) long-grain unconverted white rice, washed and drained

1½ pounds (675 g) medium shrimps, unshelled (weighed without heads)

12 ounces (340 g) tomatoes, finely chopped (about 2 cups/500 ml)

2 garlic cloves, finely chopped

2 heaped tablespoons roughly chopped cilantro

2 tablespoons roughly chopped chives

2 tablespoons roughly chopped mint

About 5 cups (1.25 l) water or fish broth

Salt to taste

DIRECTIONS:

Heat the olive oil in a deep—about 5 inches (13 cm) deep—flameproof casserole. Put in the shrimps and a good drizzle of salt, and stir-fry using high heat for approximately one minute. Remove using a slotted spoon and save for later. In the same oil fry the tomatoes, onion, pepper, and garlic on moderate heat until well amalgamated—about five minutes.

Mix in the rice, put in the water with salt to taste, and bring to its boiling point. Cover the pan and cook on moderate heat for approximately 8 minutes. Put in the shrimps and herbs and carry on cooking, covered, still on moderate heat, until the rice is soft—about ten minutes. The consistency must be soupy.

Nutrition: Calories 300, Carbs 29g, Fat 7g, Protein 42g, Potassium (K) 749 mg, Sodium (Na) 2.5 mg

Salmon With Roasted Salsa Verde

Preparation Time: 10 Minutes

Cooking Time: 25 Minutes

Servings: 3

Ingredients:

¼ cup minced fresh cilantro

1 (1¾ to 2 pound) skin on salmon fillet, 1½ inches thick

1 jalapeño chile, stemmed, halved, and seeded

1 poblano chile, stemmed, seeded, and chopped

1 tablespoon lime juice, plus lime wedges for serving

1 teaspoon ground coriander

2 tablespoons plus 2 teaspoons extra virgin olive oil

2 teaspoons chopped fresh oregano

3 garlic cloves, peeled

3 scallions, chopped

8 ounces tomatillos, husks and stems removed, washed well, dried, and quartered

Salt and pepper

DIRECTIONS:

Adjust oven racks to lowest position and 6 inches from broiler element and heat broiler. Coat baking sheet with aluminium foil. Toss tomatillos, poblano, jalapeño, 1 tablespoon oil, garlic, oregano, coriander, ¼ teaspoon salt, and ¼ teaspoon pepper together, then spread onto readied sheet. Broil vegetables on upper rack until tomatillos and jalapeños are browned, ten to twelve minutes, stirring once in a while.

Move broiled vegetables to blender and allow to cool slightly. Put in 2 tablespoons cilantro, scallions, lime juice, and 1 tablespoon oil and blend until the desired smoothness is achieved, approximately one minute. In the meantime, place clean rimmed baking sheet on lower oven rack and heat oven to 500 degrees.

Cut salmon crosswise into 4 fillets. Using sharp knife, make 4 or 5 shallow slashes, approximately an inch apart, through skin of each fillet, being cautious not to cut into flesh. Pat salmon dry using paper towels, rub with remaining 2 teaspoons oil, and sprinkle with salt and pepper.

Reduce oven temperature to 275 degrees and remove preheated baking sheet. Cautiously place salmon, skin side down, on baking sheet. Roast on lower rack until center is still translucent when checked with tip of paring knife and records 125 degrees (for medium rare), 9 to 13 minutes. Move salmon to plates, spoon some of sauce over top and drizzle with remaining 2 tablespoons minced cilantro. Serve with rest of the sauce and lime wedges.

Nutrition: Calories: 200 Cal, Carbs: 15 g, Fat: 8 g, Protein: 16 g, Fiber: 3 g.

Classic Crispy Fried Catfish Fillets

Preparation Time: 10 Minutes

Cooking Time: 5 Minutes

Servings: 3

Ingredients:

¾ cup yellow cornmeal

¼ cup all-purpose flour

2 teaspoons salt

1 teaspoon ground black pepper

½ teaspoon garlic powder, to taste

6 (4 ounce) catfish fillets

¼ teaspoon salt

Vegetable oil for frying

DIRECTIONS:

Mix the cornmeal, flour, salt, pepper, and garlic powder in a large shallow dish. Sprinkle the fish with ¼ teaspoon of salt, and dredge it in the cornmeal mixture, turning to coat it evenly.

Pour 1 ½ inches of oil into a deep cast-iron skillet and heat it to 350°F. Working in batches, fry the fish for 5 to 6 minutes or until it is golden brown; and drain it on paper towels. Serve hot.

Nutrition:

Calories: 237.7 Cal

Carbs: 39.2 g

Fat: 10.2 g

Protein: 6.3 g

Fiber: 1.3 g

BBQ Chicken Drumsticks

Preparation time: 10 minutes

Cooking time: 1 hr

Servings: 3

Ingredients

6 chicken drumsticks

½ cup water

1/3 cup ketchup

1/3 cup white vinegar

¼ cup brown sugar

4 tsps butter

2 tsps salt

2 tsps Worcestershire sauce, or to taste

2 tsps dry mustard

2 tsps chili powder, or to taste

DIRECTIONS:

Preheat the oven to 200 degrees C. In a baking dish, put drumsticks.

In a cup, whisk together water, ketchup, vinegar, brown sugar, butter, salt, Worcestershire sauce, mustard and chili powder; pour the drumsticks over the mixture. Aluminum foil cover.

Bake in a preheated oven until the bone is no longer pink and the juices run clear for around 1 hour, turning the chicken halfway through. 165 degrees F can be read by an instant-read thermometer inserted near the bone (74 degrees C).

Nutrition:

Calories: 201 Cal

Carbs: 27.3 g

Fat: 8.8 g

Protein: 3 g

Fiber: 1.2 g

Best Clam Chowder

Preparation time: 25 minutes

Cooking time: 25 minutes

Servings: 8

Ingredients

3 (6.5 ounce) cans minced clams

1 cup minced onion

1 cup diced celery

2 cups cubed potatoes

1 cup diced carrots

¾ cup butter

¾ cup all-purpose flour

1 quart half-and-half cream

2 tbsps red wine vinegar

1 ½ tsps salt

ground black pepper to taste

DIRECTIONS:

Drain the juice from the clams over the onions, celery, potatoes and carrots in a large skillet. Add water to cover, and cook until tender, over medium heat.

Meanwhile, melt the butter over a medium heat in a big heavy saucepan. Whisk in the flour until it's tender. Whisk in the cream and whisk continuously until smooth and thick. Stir in the clam juice and vegetables. Hot it but don't boil it.

Just prior to serving, whisk in the clams. They get tough when they cook too much. Stir in the vinegar when the clams are heated, and season with salt and pepper.

Nutrition: Calories: 188Kcal Carbohydrates: 1g Proteins: 11g Fat: 15g

Tiramisu

Preparation time: 35 minutes

Cooking time: 10 minutes

Servings: 12

Ingredients

6 egg yolks

¾ cup white sugar

2/3 cup milk

1 ¼ cups heavy cream

½ tsp vanilla extract

1 pound mascarpone cheese, at room temperature

¼ cup strong brewed coffee, at room temperature

2 tbsps rum

2 (3 ounce) packages ladyfinger cookies

1 tbsp unsweetened cocoa powder

DIRECTIONS:

Whisk together the egg yolks and sugar in a medium saucepan until well blended. Whisk in the milk and cook over medium heat until the mixture boils, stirring constantly. For 1 minute, boil gently, remove from heat and allow to cool slightly. Cover tightly and cool for 1 hour in the fridge.

Beat the cream with the vanilla in a medium bowl until stiff peaks develop.

Whisk the mascarpone until smooth, into the yolk mixture.

Combine the coffee and rum in a small mug. Break the ladyfingers and drizzle with the coffee mixture in half lengthwise.

Arrange half the soaked ladyfingers in a 7x11 inch dish at the rim. Over the ladyfingers, spread half of the mascarpone mixture, then half of the whipped cream over it. Repeat and sprinkle the layers with cocoa. Cover and refrigerate, until set, for 4 to 6 hours.

Nutrition: Calories 69 Total Carbs 18g Net Carbs 16g Protein 7g Fat 6g Sugar 7g Fiber 2g

Shepherd's Pie

Preparation time: 30 minutes

Cooking time: 20 minutes

Servings: 6

Ingredients

4 large potatoes, peeled and cubed

1 tbsp butter

1 tbsp finely chopped onion

¼ cup shredded Cheddar cheese

salt and pepper to taste

5 carrots, chopped

1 tbsp vegetable oil

1 onion, chopped

1 pound lean ground beef

2 tbsps all-purpose flour

1 tbsp ketchup

¾ cup beef broth

¼ cup shredded Cheddar cheese

DIRECTIONS:

To a boil, put a big pot of salted water. Add the potatoes and cook for about 15 minutes, until tender but still strong. Mash and drain. Mix the butter, the finely chopped onion and 1/4 cup of shredded cheese together. To taste, season with salt and pepper; set aside.

To a boil, put a big pot of salted water. Add the carrots and cook for about 15 minutes, until tender but still strong. Mash, drain and set aside. Preheat the oven to 375°F (190 degrees C.)

In a large frying pan, heat the oil. Add the onion, then cook until it is clear. Attach ground beef and cook until browned well. Pour off the excess fat, add the flour and cook for 1 minute. Add beef broth and ketchup. Boil, reduce heat and simmer for 5 minutes. Bring to a boil.

Spread the ground beef on the bottom of a 2 quart casserole dish in an even layer. Spread out a layer of mashed carrots next. Sprinkle with the remaining melted cheese and finish with the mashed potato mixture.

Bake for 20 minutes or until golden brown, in the preheated oven.

Nutrition: Calories 194 Total Carbs 12g Net Carbs 10g Protein 5g Fat 14g Sugar 9g Fiber 2g

Lentil Loaf

Preparation Time: 10 Minutes

Cooking Time: 55 Minutes

Servings: 3

Ingredients:

2 cups water

1 cup green lentils

2 Tbs ground flaxseeds + 4 Tbs water

1 medium yellow onion, diced

1 tsp. olive oil

1 cup instant or regular rolled oats

1 cup tomato sauce

1 tsp. garlic powder

1 tsp. dried basil

1 tsp. dried parsley

½ tsp. salt

¼ tsp. black pepper

¼ cup BBQ sauce

2 Tbs ketchup

DIRECTIONS:

Bring water to a boil.

Add lentils and simmer 25 – 30 minutes, until lentils are soft and water is evaporated.

Drain any excess water and partially mash lentils.

Scrape into mixing bowl and allow to cool slightly.

Mix flaxseeds and water together and let sit for about 15 minutes.

Sauté onion in oil over medium heat.

Cook for 5 minutes or until onion is translucent.

Stir onion and oats into lentils until mixed.

Add flax mixture, tomato sauce, garlic, basil, parsley, salt, and pepper.

Mix well.

Spoon into loaf pan that has been generously sprayed with non-stick spray.

Smooth top with back of a spoon.

Top with BBQ sauce and ketchup.

Bake at 350 degrees for about 45 minutes until top is dry, firm, and golden brown.

Let cool in pan for about 10 minutes.

Nutrition: calories 200, fat 3, fiber 6, carbs 14, protein 6

Mini Cheddar And Green Onion Quiches

Preparation Time: 10 Minutes

Cooking Time: 30 Minutes

Servings: 3

INGREDIENTS:

Pie Pastry for 2-Crust Pie

2 Tablespoons Butter, melted

1 Cup Thinly Sliced Green Onion, divided

1 Cup Shredded Sharp Cheddar Cheese

3 Large Eggs

1 Teaspoon Salt

Freshly Ground Black Pepper, About 1/8 Teaspoon

1 Teaspoon Dijon or Other Spicy Mustard

1 Cup Half-and-Half, or Half Heavy Cream and Half or Whole Milk

DIRECTIONS:

Preheat oven to 400 degrees.

Spay and flour muffin pans.

Roll the pie crust out to 1/8 of an inch. Using a small biscuit cutter, cut rounds out of pie crust. (You can use a drinking glass or empty jar if you don't have a biscuit cutter.)

Place one pastry rounds in each of the cups and tamp down gently.

Brush the pastry with melted butter.

Bake for 15 minutes.

Mix the rest of the ingredients together and fill each pastry cup 2/3 full.

Dash about half teaspoon or so of green onion over each and every cup and top with shredded cheese.

Garnish with onion. Return to oven and bake for 25 minutes or until eggs are firm

Nutrition: Calories: 242 kcal Fat: 14g Carbs: 0g Protein: 27g

Pigs In A Blanket

Preparation Time: 10 Minutes

Cooking Time: 15 Minutes

Servings: 3

INGREDIENTS:

2 Cups All-Purpose Flour

1 Teaspoon Salt

1 Tablespoon Baking Powder

1/4 Teaspoon Ground Cayenne Pepper

8 Tablespoons Butter, Room Temperature

1/2 Cup Sour Cream

1 Cup finely Shredded Sharp Cheddar Cheese

2 Dozen Mini Hot Dogs

DIRECTIONS:

Begin by mixing the baking powder, flour, cayenne and the salt. Add butter and blend it well. Pour in the cream and cheese and blend again.

Cut the dough in 2 halves, make balls of them, and cover with plastic wrap. Allow to chill for an hour or so.

Preheat oven to 400 degrees and oil or line a baking sheet with parchment sheet or a silicone baking sheet.

Place one ball on a floured surface and roll to about 1/8-inch thickness. Cut into strips approximately 2 inches wide.

Put a hot dog across the dough and roll, cutting through the dough when the hot dog is fully wrapped. Place on baking sheet. Continue until all hot dogs are wrapped.

Bake for 15 minutes.

Nutrition: Calories: 419 kcal; Fat: 3.5gCarbs: 0gProteins: 26g

Tapenade

Preparation Time: 10 Minutes

Cooking Time: 35 Minutes

Servings: 3

INGREDIENTS:

1 Can (4 Ounces) chopped Ripe Olives

2 Tablespoons Capers, drained and rinsed

1 Small Clove Garlic, minced

1 Teaspoon Anchovy Paste

Olive Oil

DIRECTIONS:

In a bowl; mix the first four materials and blend it in a food processor. If you possess pestle and mortar, then use it to mix and mash. Sprinkle on oil if needed.

Eat it with bread or with sandwiches, as the dish can be worth 2 or 3 cups.

Nutrition: Calories 324, Carbs 5g, Fat 18 g, Protein 28g,

Sheet Pan Chicken Fajitas

Preparation time: 35 minutes

Cooking time: 55 minutes

Servings: 8

Ingredients

1/3 cup vegetable oil

2 tsps chili powder

1 tsp dried oregano

½ tsp garlic powder

½ tsp onion powder

½ tsp ground cumin

½ tsp salt

¼ tsp ground black pepper

1 pinch ground cayenne pepper

1 ½ pounds of chicken tenders, quartered

4 cups of sliced bell peppers, any color

1 onion, sliced

¼ cup chopped fresh cilantro

½ lime, juiced

DIRECTIONS:

In a big resealable plastic bag, combine the vegetable oil, chili powder, oregano, garlic, onion, cumin, salt, pepper and cayenne pepper. Add the chicken, bell peppers, and onion; shake to blend.

In the refrigerator, marinate the chicken mixture for 30 minutes to 2 hours.

Preheat the oven to 400° Fahrenheit (200° C). Using aluminum foil to cover a rimmed sheet tray.

Spread the mixture of chicken over the prepared plate.

Roast for 15 to 20 minutes in the preheated oven, stirring halfway through, until the chicken is no longer pink and the bell peppers soften.

Sprinkle with cilantro and pour lime juice over the mixture of chicken; toss to spread.

Tips

The magazine version of this recipe uses 1 teaspoon of chili powder, salt, and cumin each and adds 2 thinly sliced jalapeno peppers.

Cook's Notes:

Using as needed a range of bell peppers and spicy peppers.

Instead of covering the pan with aluminum foil, coat it with a non-stick cooking spray.

Nutrition: Calories 162 Total Carbs 5g Net Carbs 4g Protein 6g Fat 14g Sugar 1g Fiber 1g

Peanut Packed Coleslaw

Preparation Time: 10 Minutes

Cooking Time: 65 Minutes

Servings: 3

List of Ingredients:

½ Cup of Cilantro, Fresh and Finely Chopped

¼ Cup of Green Onions, Finely Chopped

3 Tablespoons of Vinegar, White in Color

1 tablespoon of Sesame Oil

2 Tablespoons of Mayonnaise, Your Favorite Kind

1 teaspoon of Sugar, White

1 teaspoon of Ginger, Fresh and Finely Grated

2 teaspoons of Wasabi Paste

½ teaspoons of Salt, For Taste

½ teaspoons of Pepper, For Taste

1 Pack of Coleslaw Mix, Finely Shredded

¾ Cup of Peanuts, Light and Salted

DIRECTIONS:

1. Whisk together your first 10 ingredients in a large sized bowl.

2. Then add in your fresh coleslaw mix, making sure to stir thoroughly until evenly coated.

3. Cover and place into your fridge to chill for the next 1 hour.

4. Add in your peanuts and stir until coated. Serve whenever you are ready.

Nutrition: Calories 78 Total Carbs 20g Net Carbs 17g Protein 6g Fat 6g Sugar 12g Fiber 3g

Seared Shrimp With Tomatoes, Lime, And Avocado

Preparation Time: 10 Minutes

Cooking Time: 35 Minutes

Servings: 3

Ingredients:

⅛ teaspoon sugar

¼ cup minced fresh cilantro

1 avocado, halved, pitted, and diced

1 pound tomatoes, cored, seeded, and slice into ½ inch pieces

1 tablespoon lime juice, plus lime wedges for serving

1½ pounds extra big shrimp (21 to 25 per pound), peeled and deveined

1–2 teaspoons minced canned chipotle chile in adobo sauce

2 tablespoons vegetable oil

3 garlic cloves, minced

6 scallions, white and green parts separated and cut thin

Salt and pepper

DIRECTIONS:

Toss tomatoes, scallion whites, cilantro, garlic, chipotle, and ¾ teaspoon salt together in container. In separate container, toss shrimp with sugar, ¼ teaspoon salt, and ¼ teaspoon pepper.

Heat 1 tablespoon oil in 12 inch frying pan using high heat until just smoking. Put in half of shrimp to pan in single layer and cook, without moving, until spotty brown on one side, approximately one minute.

Move shrimp to big container (they will be underdone). Repeat with remaining 1 tablespoon oil and shrimp.

Return now empty frying pan to high heat, put in tomato mixture and lime juice, and cook until tomatoes are slightly softened, approximately one minute. Mix in shrimp with any collected juices and cook until shrimp are thoroughly cooked and hot, approximately one minute. Move shrimp to big platter and drizzle with avocado and scallion greens. Serve with lime wedges.

Nutrition: Calories: 171 Cal, Carbs: 32.6 g, Fat: 2.6 g, Protein: 5.1 g, Fiber: 5.3 g.

Shredded Fish Tamiahua (Saragalla De Pescado)

Preparation Time: 10 Minutes

Cooking Time: 15 Minutes

Servings: 3

Ingredients:

¼ cup (65 ml) finely chopped white onion

¼ cup (65 ml) water

¼ teaspoon coriander seeds, crushed

½ teaspoon salt, or to taste

½-inch (1.5-cm) piece of cinnamon stick, crushed

1 small ancho chile

1 teaspoon capers, washed, strained, and roughly chopped

1½ tablespoons raisins

12 peppercorns, crushed

2 cups (500 ml) cooked and firm-fleshed shredded fish (approximately 1 pound/450 g)

2 garlic cloves

2 serrano chiles, or any fresh, hot green chile, finely chopped

3 tablespoons light olive oil

6 green olives, pitted and finely chopped

About 6 ounces (180 g) tomatoes, finely chopped (approximately 1 cup/250 ml)

DIRECTIONS:

Take away the seeds and veins from the ancho chile, cover with water, and simmer for five minutes. Soak for another five minutes, then drain and put in to the blender jar. Put in the crushed spices, salt, garlic, and water and blend, putting in more water only if required, to a loose paste.

Heat the oil in a heavy frying pan and fry the paste for approximately one minute. Put in the tomatoes, onion, serrano chiles, olives, capers, and raisins. Fry on moderate heat for approximately five minutes, stirring occasionally, for approximately five minutes. Mix in the shredded fish and cook for five minutes longer.

Tweak the seasoning and serve either hot or cold, with freshly made tortillas.

Nutrition: Calories: 125;Carbs: 5 ;Sugar: 2 ;Fat: 9 ;Protein: 16

Shrimp A La Diabla

Preparation Time: 10 Minutes

Cooking Time: 12 Minutes

Servings: 3

Ingredients:

¼ cup chopped fresh cilantro or parsley

1 (8 ounce) can tomato sauce

1 cup water

1 onion, chopped fine

1 tablespoon lime juice, plus lime wedges for serving

1 tablespoon minced canned chipotle chile in adobo sauce

2 pounds extra big shrimp (21 to 25 per pound), peeled and deveined

2 tablespoons extra virgin olive oil, plus extra for serving

2 teaspoons dried oregano

3 garlic cloves, minced

8 dried guajillo chiles, stemmed, seeded and torn into ½ inch pieces (1 cup)

Salt and pepper

DIRECTIONS:

Toast guajillo chiles in Dutch oven on moderate heat, stirring regularly, until aromatic, 2 to six minutes; move to container.

Heat oil in now empty pot over moderate high heat until it starts to shimmer Put in onion and ½ teaspoon salt and cook until tender, approximately five minutes. Mix in garlic, chipotle, and oregano and cook until aromatic, approximately half a minute. Mix in tomato sauce, water, and toasted chiles, bring to simmer, and cook until chiles become tender, approximately ten minutes.

Move mixture to blender and pulse until smooth, approximately half a minute. Return sauce to now empty pot and mix in shrimp. Cover and cook over moderate low heat until shrimp are thoroughly cooked and completely opaque, five to seven minutes.

Move shrimp to separate plates. Stir cilantro and lime juice into sauce and sprinkle with salt and pepper to taste. Ladle sauce over shrimp, sprinkle with extra oil, and serve with lime wedges.

Nutrition: Calories: 220 Cal, Carbs: 35 g, Fat: 6 g, Protein: 7 g, Fiber: 2 g.

Fried Shrimp

Preparation Time: 10 Minutes

Cooking Time: 25 Minutes

Servings: 3

Ingredients

3 cups of large, deveined and peeled shrimp

Salt and pepper

1 egg, beaten

½ cup yellow cornmeal

½ teaspoon baking powder

½ cup half and half cream

½ cup buttermilk

1 teaspoons salt

¼ teaspoon black pepper

½ teaspoon baking powder

½ teaspoon all-purpose flour

Oil to fry your shrimp

¼ teaspoon pepper

DIRECTIONS:

Start by seasoning generously your shrimp with some salt and pepper and then leave them to sit at room temperature for 10 to 15 minutes.

Combine the eggs, cornmeal, baking powder, cream, buttermilk, salt, pepper, baking powder and flour together in a mixing bowl and mix until well blended and smooth.

Heat the oil in the deep fryer until it reaches 350°F.

Dip the shrimp in the batter to coat evenly.

Fry the shrimp until they are golden. This will take around 2 minutes.

Serve the shrimp hot, with your favorite sauce.

Nutrition: Calories: 282 Fat: 23.41 Carbohydrates: 0g Protein: 16.59 Sugar: 0g

Ground Meat Marinated in Lime Juice

Preparation Time: 10 Minutes

Cooking Time: 4 hours

Servings: 3

Ingredients:

½ cup (125 ml) fresh lime juice

2 tablespoons finely chopped white onion

4 ounces (115 g) tomatoes, finely chopped (⅔ cup/165 ml)

4 serrano chiles, finely chopped

8 ounces (225 g) freshly ground sirloin, absolutely free of fat

Salt to taste

DIRECTIONS:

Combine the lime juice well into the ground meat and set it aside to "cook" in your fridge for minimum 4 hours in a nonreactive container.

Stir in the remaining ingredients and set the meat aside to season for minimum 2 hours more.

Serve with crisp tortillas, either toasted or fried.

Nutrition: Calories: 820 Fat: 41g Carbohydrates: 0g Protein: 20.99g Sugar: 0g

Chile Rubbed Roast Chicken

Preparation Time: 10 Minutes

Cooking Time: 35 Minutes

Servings: 3

Ingredients:

⅛ teaspoon cayenne pepper

¼ cup vegetable oil

¼ teaspoon ground cinnamon

¼ teaspoon ground cloves

½ teaspoon garlic powder

½ teaspoon onion powder

½ teaspoon pepper

1 (3 to 4 pound) whole chicken, giblets discarded

1 dried chipotle chile, stemmed, seeded, and torn into ½ inch pieces (1½ tablespoons)

1 tablespoon coriander seeds

1 tablespoon cumin seeds

1 tablespoon kosher salt

2 teaspoons sugar

4 dried New Mexican chiles, stemmed, seeded, and torn into ½ inch pieces (1 cup)

Lime wedges

DIRECTIONS:

Toast New Mexican and chipotle chiles, cumin seeds, and coriander seeds in 12 inch ovensafe frying pan on moderate heat, stirring regularly, until aromatic, 2 to six minutes. Move mixture to spice grinder and allow to cool slightly. Put in pepper, onion powder, garlic powder, cloves, cinnamon, and cayenne to grinder and pulse until crudely ground, 5 to 10 seconds. Move spice mixture to container and mix in oil, salt, and sugar.

Wipe out now empty frying pan, place on middle rack of oven, and heat oven to 450 degrees. Pat chicken dry using paper towels, then gently separate skin from meat. Rub 3 tablespoons spice paste underneath skin over breast, thighs, and legs. Rub remaining spice paste over top and sides of chicken (do not rub bottom of chicken). Tuck wings behind back and tie legs together loosely using a kitchen twine.

Move chicken, breast side up, to preheated frying pan in oven. Roast chicken until breast records 120 degrees and thighs register 135 degrees, twenty-five minutes to thirty-five minutes. Turn off oven and leave chicken in oven until breast records 160 degrees and thighs register 175 degrees, twenty-five minutes to thirty-five minutes.

Move chicken to carving board and allow to rest, uncovered, for fifteen minutes. Carve and serve with lime wedges.

Nutrition: Calories 247 Total Carbs 23g Protein 4g Fat 17g Sugar 20g Fiber 1g

Classic Arroz Con Pollo

Preparation Time: 10 Minutes

Cooking Time: 15 Minutes

Servings: 3

Ingredients:

¼ cup minced fresh cilantro

¼ cup water, plus extra as required

¼ teaspoon red pepper flakes

½ cup green Manzanilla olives, pitted and halved

½ cup jarred whole pimentos, cut into 2 by ¼ inch strips

½ teaspoon dried oregano

1 (8 ounce) can tomato sauce

1 onion, chopped fine

1 small green bell pepper, stemmed, seeded, and chopped fine

1 tablespoon capers, washed

1¾ cups chicken broth

2 tablespoons olive oil

3 cups medium grain white rice

4 pounds bone in chicken thighs, trimmed

5 teaspoons distilled white vinegar

6 garlic cloves, minced

Lemon wedges

Salt and pepper

DIRECTIONS:

Adjust oven rack to middle position and heat oven to 350 degrees. Mix garlic, 1 tablespoon vinegar, 1 teaspoon salt, ½ teaspoon pepper, and oregano in big container. Put in chicken, toss to coat, and marinate for fifteen minutes.

Heat 1 tablespoon oil in Dutch oven on moderate heat until it starts to shimmer Put in onion, bell pepper, and pepper flakes and cook until starting to tenderize, approximately five minutes. Mix in 2 tablespoons cilantro.

Clear center of pot and increase heat to moderate high. Put in chicken, skin side down, to center of pot and cook until outer layer of meat becomes opaque, 2 to 4 minutes per side, reducing heat if chicken starts to brown. Mix in broth, tomato sauce, and water. Bring to simmer, cover, decrease the heat to moderate low, and simmer for about twenty minutes.

Mix in rice, olives, capers, and ¾ teaspoon salt and bring to simmer. Cover pot, move to oven, and cook, stirring every ten minutes, until chicken register 175 degrees, approximately 30 minutes. (If, after twenty minutes of cooking, rice appears dry and bottom of pot starts to scorch, mix in additional ¼ cup water.)

Move chicken to cutting board; cover pot and save for later. Using 2 spoons, pull chicken into big chunks, discarding skin and bones. Put chicken in big container, toss with pimentos, remaining 2 teaspoons vinegar, remaining 1 tablespoon oil, and remaining 2 tablespoons cilantro and sprinkle with salt and pepper to taste. Put chicken on top of rice, cover, and allow it to stand until warmed through, approximately five minutes. Serve with lemon wedges.

Nutrition: Calories 120 Total Carbs 26g Net Carbs 24g Protein 3g Fat 1g Sugar 23g Fiber 2g

Duck In A Green Pumpkin Seed Mole

Preparation Time: 10 Minutes

Cooking Time: 35 Minutes

Servings: 3

Ingredients:

Cooking the duck

1 garlic clove

1 small carrot, scraped and cut

1 small white onion, cut

5- to 6-pound (2.25- to 2.75-kg) duck

6 peppercorns

Pepper to taste

Salt to taste

The duck giblets

The sauce

⅛ teaspoon cumin seeds, crushed

1 cup (250 ml) duck broth

1 cup (250 ml) tomate verde, cooked and drained

1 small bunch radish leaves

2 big romaine lettuce leaves, torn into pieces

2 cups (500 ml) reserved duck broth

2 small garlic cloves, roughly chopped

3 sprigs epazote

3 tablespoons reserved duck drippings

3 tablespoons roughly chopped white onion

3½ ounces (100 g) hulled raw pumpkin seeds (about ¾ cup/188 ml;)

5 sprigs cilantro

6 black peppercorns, crushed

6 serrano chiles, roughly chopped

Salt as required

DIRECTIONS:

Preheat your oven to 325° f (165° c).

Place the giblets with the vegetables and seasonings into a big pan, submerge them in water, and bring to its boiling point. Reduce the heat and simmer, covered, for approximately 1½ hours.

Heat a casserole well and brown the duck all over, pricking the skin (not the flesh) to render out the fat from the layer underneath it. Drain off the surplus fat occasionally and save for later. Cover the casserole with a firmly fitting lid and braise the duck, approximately forty minutes, depending on how soft the duck is.

Set the duck aside to cool a little, then cut into serving pieces. Skim the fat from the juices in the casserole and reserve and put in the juices to the giblet broth. There must be about 5 cups (1.25 l); if not, put in water to make up to that amount.

In an ungreased frying pan, toast the pumpkin seeds about five minutes, stirring them occasionally until they swell—but do not allow them to brown. Set aside to cool, then grind them in a coffee/spice grinder with the peppercorns and cumin.

Place the ground ingredients into a container and mix in the 1 cup (250 ml) broth until you have a smooth sauce. Set it aside.

Combine the tomate verde with the chiles, onion, and garlic until the desired smoothness is achieved. Put in the greens and blend a little at a time until almost smooth, and save for later.

Heat 3 tablespoons of the reserved duck fat in a casserole and fry the ground ingredients over low heat while stirring and scraping the bottom of the pan to prevent sticking (it will swiftly scorch), approximately five minutes.

Slowly mix in the mixed ingredients and cook over low heat while stirring occasionally for approximately ten minutes. Dilute with 2 cups (500 ml) of broth and carry on cooking using super low heat for ten more minutes. Adjust salt to taste.

Slowly put in the remaining broth. Allow the sauce heat through, still using super low heat. When it is cooked, the mole should cover rather thickly the back of a wooden spoon. Put in the duck pieces and just warm them through.

Serve instantly.

Nutrition: Calories 135 Total Carbs 5g Net Carbs 4g Protein 12g Fat 8g Sugar 3g Fiber 1g

CHAPTER 2: SOUPS

Beef Stew with Herbs and Wine

Preparation Time: 5 minutes

Cooking time: 55 minutes

Servings: 4

Ingredients:

2 tbsp. olive oil

2 pounds beef stew meat, boneless, and cut into bite-sized cubes

1 tsp. smoked paprika

1 red onion, chopped

1 pound gold potatoes, peeled and diced

2 carrots, sliced

3 cloves garlic, minced

2 tomatoes, pureed

2 cups beef bone broth

½ cup dry red wine

2 bay leaves

2 thyme sprigs

2 rosemary sprigs

Salt and pepper, to taste

DIRECTIONS:

Heat olive oil in a heavy-bottomed saucepan over medium-high heat.

Add the meat, and brown for about 4 minutes until no longer pink.

Set the meat aside, and season with salt, pepper, and smoked paprika.

Add the vegetables to the pot, and continue to sauté for about 5 minutes or until crispy.

Return the meat to the pot. Add the pureed tomatoes, beef stock, red wine, bay leaves, thyme, and rosemary, and bring to a boil. When it boils, reduce the heat to low, and simmer partially covered for 50 minutes.

Distribute the stew into bowls, and serve.

Nutrition: calories: 122 fat: 7.4 g, carbs: 10.8 g protein: 3.9 g.

Chicken Soup

Preparation Time: 15 minutes

Cooking time: 45 minutes

Servings: 4

Ingredients:

1-pound whole chicken, boneless and chopped into small chunks

½ cup onions, chopped

½ cup rutabaga, cubed

2 carrots, peeled

2 celery stalks

1 cup chicken bone broth

½ tsp. ginger-garlic paste

½ cup taro leaves, roughly chopped

1 tbsp. fresh coriander, chopped

3 cups water

1 tsp. paprika

Salt and black pepper, to taste

DIRECTIONS:

In a saucepan, combine all ingredients and bring to a boil over high heat. When it boils, lower the heat and simmer, partially covered, for 40 minutes. Distribute among plates and serve immediately.

Note: You can store the soup in four airtight containers in the refrigerator for up to 3 days or in the freezer for about 6 months.

Nutrition: calories: 122 fat: 7.4 g, carbs: 10.8 g protein: 3.9 g.

Chickpea and Red Lentil Soup

Preparation Time: 5 minutes

Cooking time: 25 minutes

Servings: 4

Ingredients:

2 tsps. cumin seeds

2/5 tsps. dried chili flakes

1 tbsps. olive oil

1 red or white onion, chopped

1 cup red lentils

2 cups liquid salt-reduced vegetable stock

1 ½ cups water

14oz can chopped tomatoes

14oz can chickpeas, drained, rinsed

3 tbsps. fresh coriander, chopped, plus extra, to garnish (optional)

4 tbsps. reduced-fat Greek yogurt

DIRECTIONS:

Heat a nonstick skillet for a few minutes. Add the cumin seeds, and chili flakes, and toast for 1 minute.

Add the oil, and onion, and cook for 5 minutes. Add the lentils, broth, water, and tomatoes, and bring to a boil.

Simmer for 15 minutes until lentils soften.

Using an immersion blender, blend the soup until it is a coarse puree. Add the chickpeas, ½ cup boiling water, and continue cooking for another 5 minutes.

Add the coriander, and season to taste. Distribute into bowls, garnish with a spoonful of yogurt, and extra coriander, and serve.

Nutrition: Calories 250 Fat 7.6 g Carbs 41.8 g Protein 4.5 g

Chili Lamb Stew

Preparation Time: 10 minutes

Cooking time: 15 minutes

Servings: 4

Ingredients:

2 tbsp. olive oil

1 onion, chopped

1 lb. lamb stew, ground

Salt and black pepper to taste

2 garlic cloves, minced

1 tbsp. chili paste

2 tbsp. balsamic vinegar

¼ cup chicken stock

¼ cup mint, chopped

DIRECTIONS:

In a skillet, heat the olive oil over medium heat, and cook the onion for 3 minutes. Add the lamb stew, and cook for another 3 minutes.

Add salt, pepper, garlic, chili paste, vinegar, broth, and mint, and cook for another 6 minutes. Distribute among bowls, and serve immediately.

Nutrition: Calories 250 Fat 7.6 g Carbs 41.8 g Protein 4.5 g

Crab Stew

Preparation Time: 10 minutes

Cooking time: 15 minutes

Servings: 2

Ingredients:

1 tbsp. olive oil

¼ onion, chopped

½ tsp garlic, chopped

½ lb lump crab meat

2 cups fish stock

½ lb shrimp shelled and chopped

1 celery stalk, chopped

Salt and pepper

2 tbsps. heavy cream

DIRECTIONS:

Heat the oil in a saucepan. Add the onion, and sauté for 3 minutes. Add the garlic, and sauté for 30 seconds. Add the remaining ingredients, except the heavy cream, and mix well. Cook covered over medium heat for 25 minutes.

Add the heavy cream, stir, and serve.

Nutrition: calories: 26, sodium: 262 mg, dietary fiber: 0.7 g, total fat: 0.3 g, total carbs: 6 g, protein: 0.5 g

Cream of Mushrooms

Preparation Time: 5 minutes

Cooking time: 20 minutes

Servings: 4

Ingredients:

1 tbsp. olive oil

1 onion, finely chopped

1 lb. Champignons, peeled and cleaned

Salt and black pepper, to taste

1 lb. Cream 20% fat

DIRECTIONS:

In a skillet, heat the olive oil over medium heat. Add the onion, and sauté for a few minutes. Add the mushrooms, and cook until the water evaporates. Season with salt and pepper.

Add the cream, and bring to a boil, and serve.

Nutrition: calories: 39, sodium: 220 mg, dietary fiber: 0 g, total fat: 2.4 g, total carbs: 1.1 g, protein: 3.7 g.

Kale & Bean Soup With Chorizo

Preparation Time: 10 minutes

Cooking Time:45 Minutes

Servings: 3

Ingredients:

½ cup Manchego cheese, grated

1 cup canned Borlotti beans, drained

2 tbsp olive oil

1 lb Spanish chorizo, sliced

1 carrot, chopped

1 yellow onion, chopped

1 celery stalk, chopped

2 garlic cloves, minced

½ lb kale, chopped

4 cups chicken stock

1 tsp rosemary, dried

Salt and black pepper to taste

DIRECTIONS:

Warm the olive oil in a large pot over medium heat and cook the chorizo for 5 minutes or until the fat is rendered and the chorizo is browned. Add in onion and continue to cook for another 3 minutes until soft and translucent. Stir in garlic and let it cook for 30-40 seconds until fragrant. Lastly, add the carrots and celery and cook for 4-5 minutes until tender.

Now, pour in the chicken stock, drained and washed beans, rosemary, salt, and pepper and bring to a boil. Reduce the heat to low, cover the pot and simmer for 30 minutes. Stir periodically, checking to make sure there is enough liquid. Five minutes before the end, add the kale. Adjust the seasoning. Ladle your soup into bowls and serve topped with Manchego cheese.

Nutrition: calories: 16, sodium: 104 mg, dietary fiber: 0.8 g, total fat: 0.2 g, total carbs: 3 g, protein: 1.1 g.

Greens, Fennel, And Pear Soup With Cashews

Preparation Time: 10 minutes

Cooking Time: 15 Minutes

Servings:6

Ingredients:

2 tablespoons olive oil

1 fennel bulb, cut into ¼-inch-thick slices

2 leeks, white part only, sliced

2 pears, peeled, cored, and cut into ½-inch cubes

1 teaspoon sea salt

¼ teaspoon freshly ground black pepper

½ cup cashews

2 cups packed blanched spinach

3 cups low-sodium vegetable soup

DIRECTIONS:

Heat the olive oil in a stockpot over high heat until shimmering.

Add the fennel and leeks, then sauté for 5 minutes or until tender.

Add the pears and sprinkle with salt and pepper, then sauté for another 3 minutes or until the pears are soft.

Add the cashews, spinach, and vegetable soup. Bring to a boil. Reduce the heat to low. Cover and simmer for 5 minutes.

Pour the soup in a food processor, then pulse until creamy and smooth.

Pour the soup back to the pot and heat over low heat until heated through.

Transfer the soup to a large serving bowl and serve immediately.

Nutrition: calories: 7, sodium: 338 mg, dietary fiber: 0 g, total fat: 0 g, total carbs: 1.8 g, protein: 0.2 g.

Creamy Carrot Soup

Preparation Time: 10 minutes

Cooking time: 45 minutes

Servings: 6

Ingredients:

2 tbsps. olive oil

2 lb. carrots, peeled and sliced

½ tsp ground cumin

¼ tsp ground coriander

4 garlic cloves, chopped

2 leeks, sliced

4 cups vegetable stock

Salt and pepper

DIRECTIONS:

Heat olive oil in a saucepan over medium heat. Add carrots, cumin, coriander, garlic, leek, pepper, and salt, and cook for 15 minutes. Add broth, stir well, and bring to a boil.

Lower heat, and simmer for 30 minutes.

Using an immersion blender, puree the soup until smooth. Divide among bowls, and serve.

Nutrition: calories: 6, sodium: 0 mg, dietary fiber: 0.6 g, total fat: 0 g, total carbs: 1.2 g, protein: 0.3 g.

Creamy Kale and Mushrooms

Preparation Time: 15 minutes

Cooking time: 15 minutes

Servings: 3

Ingredients:

3 tbsps. coconut oil

3 cloves of garlic, minced

1 onion, chopped

5 white button mushrooms, chopped

Salt and pepper to taste

1 bunch kale, stems removed, and leaves chopped

1 cup of coconut milk

DIRECTIONS:

Heat the oil in a saucepan. Sauté the garlic, and onion for 2 minutes. Add the mushrooms, season with pepper, and salt, and cook for 8 minutes. Add the kale, and coconut needed, add more salt, and serve.

Nutrition: calories: 108, sodium: 5 mg, dietary fiber: 1.3 g, total fat: 7.9 g, total carbs: 9.4 g, protein: 1.9 g.

Creamy Green Garden Soup

Preparation Time: 15 minutes

Cooking time: 45 minutes

Servings: 6

Ingredients:

1 large bunch kale or green chard, preferably organic (about 1 pound)

14 cups gently packed spinach or baby cooking greens, like chard (about 12 ounces)

2 tbsps. extra-virgin olive oil, plus more for garnish

2 large yellow onions, chopped

1 tsp salt, divided

2 tbsps. plus 3 cups water, divided

¼ cup arborio rice, rinsed

4 cups vegetable broth

A pinch of cayenne pepper, to taste

1 tbsp. lemon juice, or more to taste

DIRECTIONS:

Remove the ribs from the chard or kale, and set aside. Coarsely chop the kale leaves.

Cut off the tough stems of the spinach or baby greens, and coarsely chop the leaves.

In a large skillet, heat 2 tbsps. of the oil over medium-high heat. Add the onions, and ¼ tsp salt, and cook for 5 minutes, stirring often, until the onions begin to brown.

Reduce the heat to low, add 2 tbsps. of water, and cover the pan. Cook for about 25 minutes, until onions are greatly reduced, and have a caramel color.

Meanwhile, in a saucepan, combine the remaining 3 cups water, and ¾ tsp salt, the rice, and bring the water to a boil. Reduce heat, and cook covered for 15 minutes. Add the chard or kale, and continue to simmer covered for 10 minutes.

When the onions are caramelized, stir in some of the cooking liquid. Add the onion mixture to the rice along with the spinach, vegetable broth, and cayenne. Return to a simmer, cover, and cook for 5 minutes.

Using an immersion blender, reduce the soup to a puree. Add 1 tbsp. lemon juice, and adjust salt and pepper. Distribute soup among bowls, and garnish with a drizzle of olive oil.

Note: You can serve the soup over cooked rice, and chickpeas for a more complete meal.

Nutrition: calories: 21, sodium: 539 mg, dietary fiber: 1.9 g, total fat: 0.5 g, total carbs: 4.6 g, protein: 0.6 g.

Chicken Bean Soup

Preparation Time: 10 minutes

Cooking Time:40 Minutes

Servings: 3

Ingredients:

3 tbsp olive oil

3 garlic cloves, minced

1 onion, chopped

3 tomatoes, chopped

4 cups chicken stock

1 lb chicken breasts, cubed

1 red chili pepper, chopped

1 tbsp fennel seeds, crushed

14 oz canned white beans

1 lime, zested and juiced

Salt and black pepper to taste

2 tbsp parsley, chopped

DIRECTIONS:

Warm the olive oil in a pot over medium heat. Cook the onion and garlic, adding a splash of water, for 10 minutes until aromatic. Add in the chicken and chili pepper and sit-fry for another 6-8 minutes. Put in tomatoes, chicken stock, beans, lime zest, lime juice, salt, pepper, and fennel seeds and bring to a boil; cook for 30 minutes. Serve topped with parsley.

Nutrition: calories: 237 fat: 11.7g protein: 12.3g carbs: 27.7g

Creamy Tomato and Carrot Soup

Preparation Time: 10 minutes

Cooking time: 10 minutes

Servings: 6

Ingredients:

¼ cup olive oil

1 onion, chopped

4 large carrots, peeled and chopped

4 oz can tomato, diced

1 cup vegetable broth

1 tbsp dried basil

Salt and pepper

½ cup heavy cream

DIRECTIONS:

Heat the olive oil in a saucepan. Add the onion, and carrots, and sauté for 5 minutes. Add the rest of the ingredients, except the heavy cream, and mix well. Cook covered over medium heat for 15 minutes.

Add the heavy cream, and blend the soup with an immersion blender until smooth. Distribute into bowls, and serve.

Nutrition: calories: 54, sodium: 329 mg, dietary fiber: 0 g, total fat: 1.2 g, total carbs: 4.6 g, protein: 5.8 g.

Pork & Mushroom Stew

Preparation Time: 10 minutes

Cooking Time:50 Minutes

Servings: 3

Ingredients:

2 pork chops, bones removed and cut into pieces

1 cup crimini mushrooms, chopped

2 large carrots, chopped

½ tsp garlic powder

Salt and black pepper to taste

2 tbsp butter

1 cup beef broth

1 tbsp apple cider vinegar

2 tbsp cornstarch

DIRECTIONS:

Preheat your Instant Pot on Sauté mode. Season the meat with salt and pepper. Add butter and pork chops to the pot and brown for 10 minutes, stirring occasionally. Add mushrooms and cook for 5 minutes. Add the remaining ingredients and seal the lid. Cook on High Pressure for 25 minutes. Do a quick release and serve hot.

Nutrition: calories: 51, sodium: 27 mg, dietary fiber: 0 g, total fat: 1.7 g, total carbs: 0 g, protein: 8.3 g.

Paprika Ham & Green Lentil Soup

Preparation Time: 10 minutes

Cooking Time:30 Minutes

Servings: 4

Ingredients:

2 tbsp olive oil

½ lb ham, cubed

1 onion, chopped

2 tsp parsley, dried

1 potato, chopped

3 garlic cloves, chopped

Salt and black pepper to taste

1 carrot, chopped

½ tsp paprika

½ cup green lentils, rinsed

4 cups vegetable stock

3 tbsp tomato paste

2 tomatoes, chopped

DIRECTIONS:

Warm the olive oil in a pot over medium heat and cook ham, onion, carrot, and garlic for 4 minutes. Stir in tomato paste, paprika, and tomatoes for 2-3 minutes. Pour in lentils, vegetable stock, and potato and bring to a boil. Cook for 18-20 minutes. Adjust the seasoning with salt and pepper and sprinkle with parsley. Serve warm.

Nutrition: calories: 61, sodium: 16 mg, dietary fiber: 0 g, total fat: 1.6 g, total carbs: 4.3 g, protein: 7.3 g.

Fish Stew with Tomatoes and Olives

Preparation Time: 5 minutes

Cooking time: 15 minutes

Servings: 4

Ingredients:

1 ½ lb. halibut fillet

Sat and pepper to taste

1 tbsp. olive oil

2 cloves garlic, minced

1 cup cherry tomatoes, sliced in half

3 cups tomato soup

1 cup green olives, pitted and sliced

DIRECTIONS:

Season the fish with salt and pepper.

Heat 1 tbsp. olive oil in a saucepan. Add garlic, and sauté 30 seconds. Add the fish, and cook for 3 minutes per side. Add the rest of the ingredients, and cook covered for 12 minutes. Serve hot.

Nutrition: calories: 56, sodium: 50 mg, dietary fiber: 0 g, total fat: 1.4 g, total carbs: 4.2 g, protein: 6.1 g.

Paprika Bean Soup

Preparation Time: 10 minutes

Cooking Time:50 Minutes

Servings: 3

Ingredients:

2 tbsp olive oil

6 cups veggie stock

1 cup celery, chopped

1 cup carrots, chopped

1 yellow onion, chopped

2 garlic cloves, minced

½ cup navy beans, soaked

2 tbsp chopped parsley

½ tsp paprika

1 tsp thyme

Salt and black pepper to taste

DIRECTIONS:

Warm olive oil in a saucepan and sauté onion, garlic, carrots, and celery for 5 minutes, stirring occasionally. Stir in paprika, thyme, salt, and pepper for 1 minute. Pour in broth and navy beans. Bring to a boil, then reduce the heat and simmer for 40 minutes. Sprinkle with parsley and serve.

Nutrition: calories: 36, sodium: 166 mg, dietary fiber: 0 g, total fat: 1.4 g, total carbs: 1.3 g, protein: 4.7 g.

Green Beans Soup

Preparation Time: 15 minutes

Cooking time: 40 minutes

Servings: 4

Ingredients:

½ onion, diced

1/3 cup green beans, soaked

3 cups of water

½ sweet pepper, chopped

2 potatoes, chopped

1 tbsp. fresh cilantro, chopped

1 tsp. chili flakes

DIRECTIONS:

Place all ingredients in the saucepan, and cook covered over medium heat for 40 minutes. Distribute the soup into bowls, and serve.

Nutrition: calories: 38 fat: 0.3g protein: 1.2g carbs: 9g

Grilled Tomatoes Soup

Preparation Time: 15 minutes

Cooking time: 5 minutes

Servings: 4

Ingredients:

2-pounds tomatoes

1 tbsp. avocado oil

½ cup shallot, chopped

½ tsp. ground black pepper

¼ tsp. minced garlic

1 tbsp. dried basil

3 cups low-sodium chicken broth

DIRECTIONS:

Preheat the grill to 390°F.

Cut the tomatoes in half, and grill for 1 minute on each side; then transfer to a blender, and blend until smooth.

Heat the avocado oil in a saucepan. Add the shallot, and sauté it. Add the blended grilled tomatoes, ground black pepper, minced garlic, and broth, and bring the soup to a boil. Sprinkle with the dried basil, and simmer the soup for another 2 minutes. Distribute into bowls, and serve.

Nutrition: Calories 389 Fat 6.4 g Carbs 22.9 g Protein 49.3 g

CHAPTER 3: APPETIZERS, SALADS,

SAUCES AND DRESSINGS

Horseradish Bread Sauce

Preparation Time: 10 Minutes

Cooking Time: 35 Minutes

Servings: 3

Ingredients:

1 generous tablespoon butter salt to taste

2 cups cold meat stock

2 tablespoons finely grated fresh horseradish

2 tablespoons milk

2 tender rolls or 4 slices white bread, with crusts

DIRECTIONS:

Cut bread into little pieces and soak in cold stock until it falls apart completely. Cook over medium heat and allow it to come to its boiling point; simmer 5 to 1o minutes, or until a smooth, thick sauce results.

Mix in rest of the ingredients and heat two or three minutes, but do not boil. Serve with boiled beef or tongue.

HORSERADISH SAUCE (Meerrettichsosse)

Follow recipe for White Sauce. Use beef stock and a little milk, putting in to it grated pulp of ¼ fresh horseradish root. Stir through, heat but do not boil.

Sprinkle with salt, sugar and/or lemon juice, if you think it required. A little heavy sweet cream can be swirled in just before you serve. Serve with boiled beef, tongue or chicken.

LOBSTER OR CRAB SAUCE (Hummer- oder Krabbensosse)

Put in 1 cup cooked, diced lobster meat or 1 cup crabmeat, cooked and picked-over, to basic White Sauce, and allow it to simmer. Flavor it with a little madeira and 1 tablespoon paprika. Begin to become thick with egg-yolk-cream mixture, if you wish to.

For a stronger shellfish flavor, the raw, diced crab or lobster meat can be cooked right in sauce, but in that case simmer for fifteen minutes, or until shellfish meat is meticulously cooked. Serve over steamed fish, boiled chicken, cauliflower or asparagus. This sauce can also be made with Crab Butter.

MEDIUM BROWN SAUCE (Mitteifarhene Sosse)

Follow recipe for White Sauce (above), but sauté onion until it starts to take on a light golden-brown color.

Put in flour and sauté slowly until it turns cocoa tan.

Use white or brown stock, not milk, as the liquid. This sauce is frequently seasoned with 1 tablespoon well-drained capers, white wine, lemon juice and sugar.

MUSHROOM CREAM SAUCE (Champignonsosse)

Follow recipe for White Sauce, and put in ¼ pound mushrooms cut and lightly sautéed in butter about five minutes. Simmer twenty minutes.

This sauce may then be thickened with the egg-yolk-cream mixture and seasoned with a dash of lemon juice after sauce has been taken off the heat.

Nutrition: Calories: 260;Carbs: 9 ;Sugar: 2 ;Fat: 2 ;Protein: 49

Southern-Style Collard Greens

Preparation Time: 10 Minutes

Cooking Time: 2 hours

Servings: 3

Ingredients

2 smoked ham hocks

2 sweet onions, finely chopped

3 containers of chicken broth (32 ounces each)

4 cloves of garlic, finely chopped

3 packages of collard greens (1 pound each)

2 tablespoons white vinegar

1 ½ teaspoons salt

¾ teaspoon black pepper

2 tablespoons white sugar

⅓ cup vinegar

DIRECTIONS:

Combine the garlic, onions, and ham hocks in a stockpot. Add the chicken broth and cook the mixture over medium to low heat until the meat is tender and starts to fall off the bone, about 2 hours.

Stir the collard greens, salt, black pepper, sugar, and vinegar into the broth mixture, and cook until the greens have reached the desired texture and tenderness, about 2 hours. Serve hot.

Nutrition: Calories: 310;Carbs: 20 ;Sugar: 3 ;Fat: 5 ;Protein: 27

Pickled Green Tomatoes

Preparation Time: 10 Minutes

Cooking Time: 35 Minutes

Servings: 3

Ingredients

5 pounds green tomatoes, chopped

2 tablespoons pickling salt

1 large onion, chopped

2 cups cider vinegar

1 ½ cups firmly packed brown sugar

2 teaspoons celery seed

2 teaspoons whole allspice

2 teaspoons mustard seeds

½ teaspoon whole cloves

3 cups water

DIRECTIONS:

Season the tomatoes and onions with pickling salt, and let stand for 4 to 7 hours.

Drain the ingredients and pat dry with paper towels, set aside.

In a Dutch oven, combine vinegar and brown sugar, and cook over medium heat. Stir constantly until the brown sugar dissolves.

Place the celery seed, allspice, mustard seeds, and whole cloves in a 6 inch square of cheesecloth, and tie it with a string.

Add the spice bag, along with the tomatoes, onions, and 3 cups of water to the vinegar mixture.

Bring the ingredients to a boil, stirring constantly. Reduce the heat and allow the mixture to simmer, stirring occasionally, for 25 minutes, until the onions and tomatoes are tender.

Remove and discard the spice bag.

Pour the hot pickles into mason jars, tap the jars to remove any air bubbles, and cover the jar with the metal lid.

Process in boiling water bath for at least 10 minutes.

Nutrition: Calories 48, Total Carbs 4g Net Carbs 2g Protein 1g Fat 4g Sugar 2g Fiber 2g

Fresh Broccoli Salad

Preparation time: 15 minutes

Cooking time: 15 minutes

Servings: 9

Ingredients

2 heads fresh broccoli

1 red onion

½ pound bacon

¾ cup raisins

¾ cup sliced almonds

1 cup mayonnaise

½ cup white sugar

2 tbsps white wine vinegar

DIRECTIONS:

Put the bacon in a deep skillet and cook until evenly browned over medium-high heat. Refresh and crumble.

Cut the broccoli into pieces of the bite size and cut the onion into thin slices of the bite size. Combine your favourite nuts with the bacon, raisins, and blend well.

Mix the mayonnaise, sugar and vinegar together until smooth, to prepare the dressing. Stir in the lettuce, let it cool and serve.

Nutrition: Calories: 272Kcal Carbohydrates: 1g Proteins: 15g Fat: 22g

Fruity Curry Chicken Salad

Preparation Time: 10 Minutes

Cooking Time: 35 Minutes

Servings: 3

Ingredients

4 skinless, boneless chicken breast halves - cooked and diced

1 stalk celery, diced

4 green onions, chopped

1 Golden Delicious apple - peeled, cored and diced

1/3 cup golden raisins

1/3 cup seedless green grapes, halved

½ cup chopped toasted pecans

1/8 tsp ground black pepper

½ tsp curry powder

¾ cup light mayonnaise

DIRECTIONS:

Mix the chicken, celery, onion, apple, raisins, grapes, pecans, pepper, curry powder and mayonnaise in a big bowl. Mix all together. Just serve!

Nutrition: Calories 120 Total Carbs 15g Net Carbs 13g Protein 4g Fat 5g Sugar 3g Fiber 2g

Brown Sauce

Preparation Time: 10 Minutes

Cooking Time: 35 Minutes

Servings: 3

Ingredients:

1 small onion, thoroughly minced

2 cups cold brown stock

4 tablespoons butter

4 tablespoons flour

salt to taste

DIRECTIONS:

Melt butter in a 6-cup deep cooking pan and in it sauté flour slowly, stirring continuously until it starts to brown.

Put in thoroughly minced onion, sauté a few seconds until onion starts to brown and flour has become a deeper brown.

Mix in cold stock all at once, beating with a wire whisk until the desired smoothness is achieved and well mixed. Cover and simmer thirty minutes. Season to your preference.

BROWN ONION SAUCE (Dunkle Zwiebelsosse)

Follow recipe for Brown Sauce, using 2 moderate-sized onions thoroughly minced. Just before you serve, sprinkle with salt, sugar and a little vinegar and/or red wine.

This can also be made using 3 tablespoons bacon fat instead of butter. It is then seasoned with a dash of vinegar and served over boiled potatoes. If a little beer makes up part of cooking liquid, this becomes an excellent sauce for fried Bratwurst.

Nutrition: Calories 162 Total Carbs 16g Net Carbs 12g Protein 9g Fat 5g Sugar 5g Fiber 4g

Beer Horseradish Sauce

Preparation Time: 10 Minutes

Cooking Time: 35 Minutes

Servings: 3

Ingredients:

½ cup water or sweet cream

1 cup dark or light beer (dark gives the sauce a richer flavor and better color)

2 egg yolks

2 tablespoons butter or bacon fat

2 tablespoons flour

2 tablespoons grated horseradish root

salt, prepared sharp mustard, pepper to taste

sweet cream or sour cream (not necessary)

DIRECTIONS:

Melt butter in a 1-quart deep cooking pan and in it sauté flour until medium brown. Slowly mix in cold beer, beating as you do so to keep sauce smooth.

Simmer ten minutes. Put in grated horseradish, salt, mustard and pepper and mix thoroughly. Sauce may be kept hot using low heat, but do not allow it to boil once more.

Beat egg yolks into cool water or sweet cream. Put in slowly about ½ cup of the hot sauce to egg-yolk mixture, and when mixed, turn this back into rest of the sauce. Stir and heat, but do not boil.

If you mixed egg yolks with water, sauce may be finished with a tablespoonful or two of sweet or sour cream. Well-drained bottled horseradish sauce can be used for this, but in that case do not put in any cream and flavor with a little sugar.

Nutrition: Calories 121 Total Carbs 6g Net Carbs 5g Protein 3g Fat 9g Sugar 4g Fiber 1g

Curry Sauce

Preparation Time: 10 Minutes

Cooking Time: 35 Minutes

Servings: 3

Ingredients:

1 cup hot stock (chicken veal or beef, depending on the food to be served with the sauce)

1 scant cup hot milk

1 small onion, thoroughly minced

1 to 1½ teaspoons curry powder

2 moderate-sized tart apples, peeled and diced

3 to 4 tablespoons dry white wine

4 tablespoons butter

4 tablespoons flour

4 tablespoons sour cream

salt to taste

DIRECTIONS:

Melt butter in a 6-cup deep cooking pan and in it sauté onion slowly until tender and pale golden in color. Drizzle flour into butter and sauté, stirring continuously using low heat, until flour is pale cocoa color. Put in diced and peeled apples, drizzle with curry powder and sauté together for two or three minutes. Mix in hot stock and milk.

Cover and simmer gently fifteen to twenty minutes, or until apple is tender enough to mash. Strain sauce through a fine sieve and return to pan. Season to your preference with salt, sour cream and white wine. Heat for a few seconds but do not boil. This is excellent with boiled chicken and rice, or with grilled pork or lamb chops.

Nutrition: Calories 143 Total Carbs 6g Protein 4g Fat 12g Sugar 5g Fiber 0g

Chunky Guacamole

Preparation Time: 10 Minutes

Cooking Time: 35 Minutes

Servings: 3

Ingredients:

¼ cup minced fresh cilantro

½ teaspoon ground cumin

1 jalapeño chile, stemmed, seeded, and minced

2 garlic cloves, minced

2 tablespoons finely chopped red onion

2 tablespoons lime juice

3 ripe avocados

Salt

DIRECTIONS:

Halve 1 avocado, remove pit, and scoop flesh into moderate container. Put in cilantro, jalapeño, onion, lime juice, garlic, ¾ teaspoon salt, and cumin and purée with potato masher (or fork) until mostly smooth.

Halve, pit, and dice remaining 2 avocados. Put in cubes to container with mashed avocado mixture and gently purée until mixture is well blended but still coarse. (Guacamole can be placed in your fridge for maximum one day using plastic wrap pressed directly against its surface.) Sprinkle with salt to taste before you serve.

Nutrition: Calories: 100;Carbs: 10 ;Sugar: 3 ;Fat: 6 ;Protein: 5

Empanadas

Preparation Time: 10 Minutes

Cooking Time: 35 Minutes

Servings: 3

Ingredients:

1 recipe filling, chilled

1 tablespoon sugar

1¼ cups ice water

1½ teaspoons salt

12 tablespoons unsalted butter, cut into ½ inch pieces and chilled

2 tablespoons extra virgin olive oil

3¾ cups (18¾ ounces) all-purpose flour

DIRECTIONS:

Process flour, sugar, and salt together in food processor until blended, approximately 3 seconds. Spread butter pieces over flour mixture and pulse until mixture resembles coarse cornmeal, approximately 16 pulses. Move mixture to big container. Working with ¼ cup ice water at a time, drizzle water over flour mixture and, using stiff rubber spatula, stir and press dough together until dough sticks together and no small bits of flour remain (you may not need to use all of water).

Turn dough onto clean, dry counter and softly push into consistent ball. Split dough into 2 even pieces. Turn each piece of dough onto sheet of plastic wrap, flatten into 6 inch disks, wrap firmly, and place in your fridge for an hour. Allow the chilled dough to sit on counter to tenderize slightly, approximately ten minutes, before rolling.

Adjust oven racks to upper middle and lower middle positions and heat oven to 425 degrees. Coat 2 baking sheets using parchment paper. Roll 1 dough disk into 18 inch circle, approximately ⅛ inch thick, on mildly floured counter. Using 4 inch round biscuit cutter, cut out 12 rounds, discarding dough scraps. Put 1 tablespoon filling in center of each dough round. Brush edges of dough with water and fold dough over filling. Push to secure, and crimp edges with tines of fork. Move to 1 prepared sheet, cover, and place in your fridge Repeat with the rest of the dough disk and rest of the filling. (Filled empanadas can be wrapped firmly using plastic wrap and placed in the fridge for maximum one day or frozen for maximum 1 month. After empanadas are completely frozen, approximately eight hours, they can be moved to zipper lock freezer bags to save space in freezer. Move back to parchment paper covered sheet before you bake. Increase baking time by about five minutes.)

Brush tops of empanadas with oil and bake until a golden-brown colour is achieved, twenty minutes to half an hour, switching and rotating sheets midway through baking. Allow to cool for five minutes before you serve.

Empanada Fillings

These fillings should be chilled at the time of using, and hence should be prepared in advance. Each filling makes enough for 24 empanadas.

Nutrition: Calories 320, Carbs 11g, Fat 23g, Protein 47g

Hot Corn Dip

Preparation Time: 10 Minutes

Cooking Time: 35 Minutes

Servings: 3

Ingredients

2 cups corn kernel

½ cup diced onion

2 tablespoons mayonnaise

1 ½ tablespoons butter

1 clove garlic, minced

1-2 jalapenos, seeded and diced

¼ teaspoon seasoned salt

¾ cup sharp cheddar cheese, shredded

½ cup Monterey Jack Cheese, shredded

¼ teaspoon chili powder

4 tablespoons cream cheese

1 green onion, sliced

Tortilla chips for dipping

Cooking spray

DIRECTIONS:

Preheat oven to 375°F.

In a skillet, melt butter, and add corn, onion, and jalapeño. Sauté for 3 minutes.

Add garlic and continue to sauté for 1 to 2 more minutes.

Remove the mixture from heat and allow the mixture to cool for a few minutes before adding all the remaining ingredients. Stir to combine.

Transfer to a baking dish coated with cooking spray, and bake for 20 minutes, until the cheese bubbles.

Serve with tortilla chips for dipping.

Nutrition: Calories: 235 Fat: 13g Carbohydrates: 1g Protein: 2Sugar: 1g

Dried Mushroom Sauce

Preparation Time: 10 Minutes

Cooking Time: 35 Minutes

Servings: 3

Ingredients:

½ cup hot water

½ ounce dried mushrooms

1 to 2 tablespoons sour cream (not necessary)

1½ cups water or beef stock

1½ tablespoons butter

1½ tablespoons flour

salt and pepper to taste

DIRECTIONS:

Soak mushrooms in ½ cup hot water twenty minutes. Drain water off and cut mushrooms. Cook gradually twenty-five minutes, or until soft, in water or beef stock. Melt butter in a 1-quart deep cooking pan and in it sauté flour until medium brown.

Put in stock in which mushrooms were cooked, beating continuously to keep sauce smooth. Cook sauce with mushroom pieces 5 to ten minutes and season to taste with salt and pepper. Mix in sour cream if you wish, and heat three to four minutes, but do not boil.

Nutrition: Calories: 666 kcal; Carbs: 0.3gFat: 54gProteins: 43g

Hollandaise Sauce

Preparation Time: 10 Minutes

Cooking Time: 35 Minutes

Servings: 3

Ingredients:

¼ pound butter

1 to 2 teaspoons lemon juice

4 egg yolks

salt and white pepper to taste

Worcestershire sauce, optional and to taste

DIRECTIONS:

Split butter into 4 equivalent portions. Put egg yolks in top of a twofold boiler and put in 1 portion of butter. Stir swiftly and continuously, over hot but not boiling water, until butter is melted. Use a wire whisk or wooden spoon for beating.

Put in second portion of butter, and as it melts, the third, and so on, until all the butter has been melted and worked into egg yolks.

Remove pan from hot water, beat for one more minute or two and put in lemon juice, salt and pepper. In Germany, a little Worcestershire sauce is frequently added to this sauce. Put pan back over the hot (but still not boiling) water.

Heat and stir for one more minute or two before you serve. If sauce curdles as you are cooking it, put in one to two tablespoons boiling water and beat until the desired smoothness is achieved. Always make this sauce just before it is to be served.

BÉARNAISE SAUCE

This is made like Hollandaise (above), apart from that herb-flavored vinegar is substituted for lemon juice. Prepare vinegar well ahead of time so that it will be cool before you begin making the sauce.

Simmer ½ cup wine vinegar with 1 tablespoon each minced shallots or scallions and tarragon and 2 peppercorns, slightly crushed.

Simmer uncovered using low heat until vinegar is reduced to approximately 2 tablespoons. Strain and cool. Beat cooled, flavored vinegar into 3 egg yolks and using ½ pound butter, proceed with recipe. A drizzling of chopped tarragon and/or parsley can be added before you serve.

If you cannot get fresh or dried tarragon, use tarragon vinegar and simmer it down with the minced shallots.

Nutrition: Protein: 23.8 grams Carbs: 13.2 grams Fiber: 9 grams Sugar: 2.2 grams Fats: 3.5

Hot Bacon Dressing

Preparation Time: 10 Minutes

Cooking Time: 35 Minutes

Servings: 3

Ingredients:

¼ cup vinegar, or to taste

¼ teaspoon pepper

½ teaspoon salt

1½ tablespoons sugar, or to taste

6 slices bacon, diced

DIRECTIONS:

Fry diced bacon slowly in a frying pan until crunchy. Do not drain off fat. Put in vinegar, sugar, salt and pepper, heat to boiling point and stir continuously. Season to taste and put in slightly more sugar, vinegar or salt as required.

Pour while hot over warm cooked string beans or warm cut boiled potatoes. This amount of dressing is enough for a salad of 1 pound potatoes, or 1 pound string beans. Never chill this dressing, as the bacon fat will solidify.

Nutrition: Calories: 296 kcal Fat: 22.63g Carbs: 0g Protein: 21.71g

CHAPTER 4: DESSERTS AND SNACKS

Drop Sugar Pecan Cookies

Preparation Time: 10 Minutes

Cooking Time: 25 Minutes

Servings: 3

INGREDIENTS

2 1/2 cups all purpose flour

1/2 tsp. baking soda

3/4 tsp. salt

1 cup unsalted butter, softened

1 cup granulated sugar

1 tsp. vanilla extract

1 beaten egg

2 tbs. whole milk

1/2 cup chopped pecans

Colored sugars

DIRECTIONS:

1. Preheat the oven to 400°. Lightly spray your baking sheets with non stick cooking spray. In a mixing bowl, add the all purpose flour, baking soda and salt. Stir until combined.

2. In a separate mixing bowl, add the butter and granulated sugar. Using a mixer on medium speed, beat for 3 minutes. Add the vanilla extract and egg. Mix for 2 minutes. Turn the mixer off and stir in the pecans.

3. Drop the cookies, by teaspoonfuls, onto the baking sheets. Space the cookies about 2" apart. Dip the bottom of a glass in your favorite colored sugars.

4. Bake for 10 minutes or until the cookies are set and lightly browned. Remove the cookies from the baking sheets and cool completely before serving.

Nutrition: Calories 327, Carbohydrates 29g, Fiber 2g, Cholesterol 69mg, Fat 7g, Sugar 0.3g, Protein 28g

Ham Rolls With Asparagus

Preparation Time: 10 Minutes

Cooking Time: 75 Minutes

Servings: 3

Ingredients:

1 teaspoon lemon juice

12 asparagus, cooked but firm

2 cups water in which asparagus were cooked

2 envelopes unflavored gelatin

4 fine slices boiled or baked ham

two to three tablespoons mayonnaise

DIRECTIONS:

Asparagus must be thoroughly drained using paper towels and meticulously chilled. (Retain water in which it is cooked.) Spread one side of each ham slice with mayonnaise.

Lay three asparagus crosswise at one end of each ham slice. Roll ham. Each roll must then be covered with following aspic. Dissolve gelatin in ½ cup cold asparagus water. Flavor remaining water with lemon juice. Heat, take off the stove and put in softened gelatin.

Stir until it has thoroughly blended. When mixture starts to become thick slightly, and before it sets, spoon over ham and asparagus rolls which have been arranged on a big flat dish so they do not touch each other.

Put in fridge 1 hour or until meticulously set. Serve on separate salad plates, on lettuce leaves. Garnish tops of ham rolls with pimento strips or chopped hard-cooked eggs. Serve extra mayonnaise on the side.

Nutrition: Calories 106 Total Carbs 5g Net Carbs 4g Protein 7g Fat 8g Sugar 0g Fiber 1g

Jellied Calves' And Pigs' Feet

Preparation Time: 10 Minutes

Cooking Time: 15 Minutes

Servings: 3

Ingredients:

1 big onion

1 cup white vinegar

10 peppercorns

2 bay leaves

2 calves' feet

2 pigs' feet

2 tablespoons salt

water to immerse

DIRECTIONS:

Rinse calves' and pigs' feet well in several changes of water. Put in pot with water to immerse, vinegar, salt, onion, bay leaves and peppercorns. Bring to its boiling point and cook briskly 4 or five minutes, skimming surface as foam rises.

Decrease the heat and simmer slowly but steadily for about ninety minutes. Remove feet and simmer broth for another ½ hour, or until it is reduced by ⅓ to ½ its original volume. When feet are sufficiently cool to handle, pick meat from bones and place in mold or baking dish.

Strain stock through a very fine sieve or cloth, cool and skim fat from surface. Taste for seasoning and put in more vinegar if required. Pour over meat and chill until set.

To serve, unmold onto a cold platter, or simply cut portions from mold and place on individual salad plates. Decorate using pickled beets, gherkins, hard-cooked egg slices and freshly grated horseradish.

Nutrition: Calories 145 Total Carbs 10g Net Carbs 5g Protein 9g Fat 9g Sugar 5g Fiber 5g

Chilied Peanuts

Preparation Time: 10 Minutes

Cooking Time: 10 Minutes

Servings: 3

Ingredients:

1 cup (250 ml) raw shelled peanuts, with or without brown papery skins

1 tablespoon vegetable oil

1 teaspoon salt, or to taste

1 to 1½ teaspoons powdered chile de árbol, or to taste

10 small garlic cloves

DIRECTIONS:

In a frying pan just big enough to accommodate the peanuts in a single layer, heat the oil. Put in the peanuts and garlic cloves and fry for approximately 2 minutes, flipping them over continuously.

Reduce the heat a little, put in the powdered chile and salt, and cook for one minute or two longer, stirring occasionally to prevent sticking; take care that the chile powder does not burn.

Set aside to cool before you serve with drinks.

Nutrition: Calories 198 Total Carbs 5g Net Carbs 3g Protein 9g Fat 17g Sugar 1g Fiber 2g

Classic Margaritas

Preparation Time: 10 Minutes

Cooking Time: 15 Minutes

Servings: 3

Ingredients:

¼ cup superfine sugar

1 cup 100 percent agave tequila, if possible reposado

1 cup triple sec

2 cups crushed ice

4 teaspoons finely grated lemon zest plus ½ cup juice (3 lemons)

4 teaspoons finely grated lime zest plus ½ cup juice (4 limes)

Pinch salt

DIRECTIONS:

Mix lime zest and juice, lemon zest and juice, sugar, and salt in 2 cup liquid measuring cup; cover and place in your fridge until flavors meld, minimum 4 hours or maximum one day.

Split 1 cup crushed ice among four to 6 margarita or twofold old fashioned glasses. Strain juice mixture into 1 quart pitcher or cocktail shaker; discard solids. Put in tequila, triple sec, and remaining 1 cup crushed ice; stir or shake until meticulously blended and chilled, 20 to 60 seconds. Strain into ice filled glasses and serve instantly.

Nutrition: Calories: 120 Fat: 3.41g Carbohydrates: 0g Protein: 20.99g Sugar: 0g Cholesterol: 65mg

Strawberry Margaritas

Preparation Time: 10 Minutes

Cooking Time: 10 Minutes

Servings: 3

Ingredients:

¼ cup superfine sugar

½ cup Chambord

½ cup lemon juice (3 lemons)

½ cup lime juice (4 limes)

1 cup 100 percent agave tequila, if possible reposado

1 cup triple sec

2 cups crushed ice

5 ounces strawberries, hulled (1 cup)

Pinch salt

DIRECTIONS:

Process strawberries, lime juice, lemon juice, sugar, and salt in blender until the desired smoothness is achieved, approximately half a minute.

Split 1 cup crushed ice among four to 6 margarita or twofold old fashioned glasses. Strain juice mixture into 1 quart pitcher or cocktail shaker; discard solids. Put in tequila, triple sec, Chambord, and remaining 1 cup crushed ice; stir or shake until meticulously blended and chilled, 20 to 60 seconds. Strain into ice filled glasses and serve instantly.

Nutrition: Calories: 89 Fat: 6.33gCarbohydrates: 0g Protein: 7.56g Sugar: 0g

Molletes

Preparation Time: 10 Minutes

Cooking Time: 15 Minutes

Servings: 3

Ingredients:

½ cup finely chopped onion

½ cup fresh cilantro leaves

1 (16 inch) loaf French or Italian bread

1 cup refried beans

1 garlic clove, minced

1 jalapeño chile, stemmed, seeded, and minced

2 tablespoons lime juice

3 tomatoes, cored and chopped

4 tablespoons unsalted butter, softened

8 ounces mild cheddar cheese, shredded (2 cups)

Salt and pepper

DIRECTIONS:

Toss tomatoes with ¼ teaspoon salt in colander and allow to drain for half an hour As tomatoes drain, layer onion, cilantro, jalapeño, and garlic on top. Shake colander to drain off and discard surplus tomato juice. Move mixture to container, mix in lime juice, and sprinkle with salt and pepper to taste.

Adjust oven rack to middle position and heat oven to 400 degrees. Coat baking sheet with aluminum foil. Slice bread in half horizontally, then remove all but ¼ inch of interior crumb; reserve removed crumb for future use. Spread butter uniformly inside hollowed bread and place cut side up on prepared sheet. Bake until mildly toasted and browned, approximately eight minutes.

Allow the bread to cool slightly, spread refried beans uniformly inside toasted bread and top with cheese. Bake until cheese is just melted, five to seven minutes. Move bread to cutting board, top with salsa, and slice crosswise into 2 inch pieces. Serve warm.

Nutrition: Protein: 20 grams Carbs: 12.2 grams Fiber: 11.9 grams Sugar: 11.2 grams Fats: 7.5 grams Calories: 320

Homemade Fried Tortilla Chips

Preparation Time: 10 Minutes

Cooking Time: 15 Minutes

Servings: 3

Ingredients:

5 cups peanut oil

8 (6 inch) corn tortillas

Kosher salt

DIRECTIONS:

Cut each tortilla into 6 wedges. Coat 2 baking sheets with several layers of paper towels. Heat oil in Dutch oven over moderate high heat to 350 degrees.

Put in half of tortillas and fry until golden and crisp around edges, 2 to 4 minutes. Move fried chips to prepared sheet, drizzle lightly with salt, and allow to cool. Repeat with remaining tortillas and serve. (Cooled chips can be stored at room temperature for maximum four days.)

Nutrition: Calories: 136Fat: 3.41g Carbohydrates: 0g Protein: 20.99g Sugar: 0

Candy Bar Brownies

Preparation Time: 10 Minutes

Cooking Time: 45 Minutes

Servings: 3

INGREDIENTS

3/4 cup unsalted butter

2 cups granulated sugar

2 tsp. vanilla extract

4 eggs

1 1/2 cups all purpose flour

1/2 tsp. baking powder

1/4 tsp. salt

1/3 cup unsweetened baking cocoa

4 regular size Snickers candy bars, chopped

3 regular size Hershey's milk chocolate bars, chopped

DIRECTIONS:

1. In a sauce pan over medium heat, add the butter and granulated sugar. Stir constantly and cook until the butter and sugar melt. Remove the pan from the heat. Add the vanilla extract and eggs to the pan. Whisk until smooth and combined. Add the all purpose flour, baking powder, salt and cocoa. Whisk until the batter is smooth and combined. Add the Snickers candy bars and stir until combined.

2. Spray a 9 x 13 baking pan with non stick cooking spray. Preheat the oven to 350°. Spread the batter into the pan. Sprinkle the Hershey bars over the top. Bake for 35 minutes or until a knife inserted off center of the brownies comes out clean. Remove the brownies from the oven and cool completely before cutting.

Nutrition: Calories: 352 Fat: 29g Protein: 17g Carbs: 5g Fiber: 2gNet Carbs: 3g

Southern Crispy Fried Green Tomatoes

Preparation Time: 10 Minutes

Cooking Time: 30 Minutes

Servings: 3

Ingredients:

4 large green tomatoes

2 eggs

½ cup milk

1 cup all-purpose flour

2 teaspoons sea salt

½ teaspoon cayenne powder

½ cup cornmeal

½ cup bread crumbs

1 quart vegetable oil for frying

DIRECTIONS:

Slice the tomatoes in ½-inch thick slices. Discard the tops and bottoms.

Combine and whisk the eggs and milk together in a medium-size bowl.

Set up your dredging station, with one bowl for flour, salt, and cayenne powder, and in another, combine the cornmeal and bread crumbs.

Dip your tomatoes into the egg mixture, and roll them in the flour.

Dip again in the egg, and cover with crushed bread crumbs and cornmeal.

Pour the vegetable oil into a large saucepan, and heat over medium heat.

Working in batches, deep fry the tomatoes until they are golden brown. Remove them carefully from the hot oil with a slotted spoon, and set them aside on paper towel to drain.

Nutrition: Calories 279, Carbohydrates 30g, Cholesterol 36mg, Fiber 5g, Sugar 0.8g, Protein 25g,

Matjes Rolls

Preparation Time: 10 Minutes

Cooking Time: 35 Minutes

Servings: 3

Ingredients:

½ cup white wine

1 cup milk or buttermilk

3 tablespoons minced chives

6 matjes filets

6 tablespoons Horseradish

6 thick round slices of apple, peeled

Whipped Cream

DIRECTIONS:

Soak matjes filets in milk or buttermilk two hours. Allow apple slices to marinate in white wine thirty minutes to an hour.

Take herring fillets out of milk and drain using a paper towel.

Put 1 tablespoon Horseradish Cream into center of each filet, roll and fasten using a toothpick. Drizzle top with minced chives.

Set each roll on an apple slice that has been drained using paper towel and serve on separate plates decorated with a few slices of pickled beets and several gherkins.

Nutrition: Calories 81 Total Carbs 2g Net Carbs 1g Protein 3g Fat 7g Sugar 0g Fiber 1g

Chocolate Coconut Trifle

Preparation time: 30 minutes

Cooking time: 15 minutes

Servings: 12

Ingredients

1 (14 ounce) can sweetened condensed milk

½ (14 ounce) can coconut milk

1 ⅔ cups milk

3 egg yolks

2 tbsps cornstarch

2 ½ cups shredded coconut

½ cup unsweetened cocoa powder

¾ cup heavy whipping cream

¼ cup of milk, or as needed

15 ladyfingers

1 ¼ cups of shredded coconut

1 tbsp shaved dark chocolate

DIRECTIONS:

In a low-heat saucepan, mix sweetened condensed milk, coconut milk, milk, egg yolks, and cornstarch; cook, stirring constantly, until the custard is thickened, around 10 minutes.

Break the custard into 2 bowls. Mix the first bowl of custard with 2 1/2 cups of shredded coconut. In the second bowl of custard, fold up the cocoa powder. Let the mixture of custard cool for about 10 minutes.

Using an electric mixer to beat the cream in a chilled glass or metal bowl until soft peaks form.

In a small tub, pour in 1/4 cup of milk. Dip ladyfingers in milk briefly and place them in a glass trifle bowl at the bottom. Spoon the top of coconut custard. Layer on top of the remaining ladyfinger and chocolate custard. Over the top, smooth whipped cream.

Place 1 1/4 of a cup of shredded coconut over low heat in a small skillet. Cook and stir for 3 to 5 minutes until toasted and fragrant. Just let it cool.

Sprinkle over the whipped cream with toasted coconut and chocolate. Cover and refrigerate for about 4 hours, before the flavors melt.

Nutrition: Calories 165 Total Carbs 13g Net Carbs 12g Protein 11g Fat 7g Sugar 1g Fiber 1g

Dried Shrimp Fritters

Preparation Time: 10 Minutes

Cooking Time: 15 Minutes

Servings: 3

Ingredients:

½ cup (125 ml) finely chopped white onion

¾ cup (190 ml) small dried shrimps, cleaned

1 cup (250 ml) cold water

1 egg white

4 ounces (115 g) flour (approximately 1 scant cup)

5 serrano chiles, finely chopped

Salt to taste

Vegetable oil for frying

DIRECTIONS:

Combine the flour, water, and salt together for a couple of minutes and leave the batter to stand for minimum 1 hour.

Wash the shrimps to remove surplus salt. Cover with warm water and leave them to soak for approximately five minutes—no longer.

Beat the egg white until stiff and fold it into the batter.

Drain the shrimps (if large, cut into 2) and put in them, with the chopped onion and chiles, to the batter.

176

Heat the oil in a frying pan and drop tablespoons of the mixture into it, a few at a time. Fry the botanas until they become golden brown, flipping them over once. Drain them on the paper towelling and serve instantly.

Nutrition: Calories 270, Carbs 16g, Fat 10g, Protein 23g,

Keto Cheesecake Cupcakes

Preparation time: 10 minutes

Cooking time: 15 minutes

Servings: 12

Ingredients

½ cup almond meal

¼ cup buttcr, melted

2 (8 ounce) cream cheese containers, softened

2 eggs

¾ cup granular no-calorie sucralose sweetener

1 tsp vanilla extract

DIRECTIONS:

Preheat the oven to 350 degrees Celsius (175 degrees C). Strip 12 liners of paper muffin cups.

In a cup, mix the almond meal and butter; spoon into the paper liners' bottoms and press into a flat crust.

In a bowl with an electric mixer set to medium to smooth, beat the cream cheese, eggs, sweetener, and vanilla extract together; spoon the paper liners over the crust layer.

Bake in the preheated oven for 15 to 17 minutes until the cream cheese mixture is almost set in the centre.

Cool the cupcakes at room temperature until they are cool enough to handle them. Until serving, refrigerate for 8 hours to overnight.

 Nutrition:

Calories: 356 Cal

Carbs: 49 g

Fat: 17 g

Protein: 5.1 g

Fiber: 2.5 g

Punch Bowl Cake

Preparation Time: 10 Minutes

Cooking Time: 35 Minutes

Servings: 3

INGREDIENTS

18 oz. box yellow cake mix

2 cans cherry pie filling, 21 oz. size

4 boxes instant vanilla pudding mix, 4 serving size

8 cups whole milk

15 oz. can pineapple tidbits

4 bananas, peeled and sliced

2 tbs. lemon juice

16 oz. carton Cool Whip, thawed

1/2 cup chopped pecans

1/2 cup maraschino cherries

1/2 cup sweetened flaked coconut DIRECTIONS:

1. Prepare and bake the cake mix according to package DIRECTIONS:. Bake the cake in two 9" round cake pans. Cool the cake completely before using. Cut the cake into cubes.

2. In a large punch bowl, add half the cake cubes. Spread 1 can cherry pie filling over the cake. In a mixing bowl, add the vanilla pudding mix and milk. Using a mixer on medium speed, beat until the pudding thickens. Spread half the pudding over the cherry pie filling. Spread half the pineapple over the pudding.

3. In a mixing bowl, add the bananas and lemon juice. Toss until the bananas are coated in the lemon juice. Spread half the bananas over the pineapple. Spread half the Cool Whip over the top. Repeat the layering process one more time using the remaining cake, cherry pie filling, pudding, pineapple, bananas and Cool Whip. Sprinkle the pecans, maraschino cherries and coconut over the top. Cover the top of the punch bowl and refrigerate at least 8 hours before serving.

Nutrition: Calories 117, Carbohydrates 9g, Fiber 2g, Cholesterol 3mg, Sugar 3g, Protein 11g,

Blueberry Waffles with Fast Blueberry Sauce

Preparation time: 40 minutes

Cooking time: 20 minutes

Servings: 6

Ingredients

3 egg yolks, beaten

1 ⅔ cups milk

2 cups all-purpose flour

2 ¼ tsps baking powder

½ tsp salt

¼ cup melted butter

3 egg whites, stiffly beaten

2/3 cup blueberries

1 ½ cups blueberries

3 tbsps honey

½ cup orange juice

1 tbsp cornstarch

DIRECTIONS:

Whisk together the egg yolks and milk in a medium dish. Stir in the rice, salt and baking powder. Add the butter and set the mixture aside for approximately 30 minutes.

Preheat a waffle iron that is lightly greased.

Into the mixture, fold the egg whites and 2/3 cup blueberries. Scoop in the prepared waffle iron portions of the mixture, and cook until golden brown.

Mix 1 1/2 cups of blueberries, honey and 1/4 cup orange juice in a medium saucepan over medium heat to prepare the sauce. Just bring it to a boil. In a small cup, combine the remaining orange juice and cornstarch and whisk in the blueberry mixture. Stir continuously until it thickens. Over waffles, serve soft.

Nutrition: Calories 155 Total Carbs 16g Net Carbs 10g Protein 10g Fat 7g Sugar 7g Fiber 6g

Barbecued Chicken Wontons

Preparation Time: 10 Minutes

Cooking Time: 30 Minutes

Servings: 3

INGREDIENTS:

1 Cup Cooked Diced Chicken

1 Teaspoon Cajun Seasoning

3 Green Onions with About 3 To 4 Inches of Green, coarsely chopped

1/4 Teaspoon Salt

Dash Black Pepper

3 Tablespoons Barbecue Sauce

24 To 30 Wonton Wrappers

Oil for Deep Frying

Barbecue Sauce for Dipping

DIRECTIONS:

Chop the chicken pieces and the seasoned onions.

Add in three tablespoons of BBQ sauce and mix well.

Place one teaspoon of the chicken mix at the middle of the wonton wrap. Brush some water at all the edges of the wrapper. Fold it and seal it by pressing along the seams.

Place the completed wontons under damp paper towels to keep them moist.

Heat oil to 370 degrees in deep frying pan or electric fryer.

Fry the wonton three or four at a time until they turn golden.

Remove to a paper towel lined plate in a 200-degree oven to keep warm as they drain.

Serve with BBQ sauce.

Nutrition: Protein: 19.7grams Carbs: 26.2 grams Fiber: 21.5 grams Sugar: 0 grams Fats: 17.2

Sweet And Sour Meatballs Recipe

Preparation Time: 10 Minutes

Cooking Time: 30 Minutes

Servings: 3

INGREDIENTS:

1 1/2 Pounds Lean Ground Beef

1/3 Cup Plain Dry Bread Crumbs (fine)

1/4 Teaspoon Salt

1/2 Teaspoon Garlic Powder

1/4 Teaspoon Ground Ginger

1 Large Egg, slightly beaten

2/3 Cup Apricot Preserves, or Peach Preserves

2 Tablespoons Soy Sauce

1 Tablespoon Peanut Butter

1 Teaspoon Sesame Oil

1/4 Cup Rice Vinegar

1/2 Teaspoon Chili-Garlic Paste or About 1/4 Teaspoon Ground Cayenne Pepper

1 Red Bell Pepper, sliced

DIRECTIONS:

Preheat oven to 350 degrees, and put foil in a jelly roll or roasting pan. Spray the pan with cooking spray.

In a large bowl, mix the beef, salt, garlic, bread crumbs, eggs and the ginger. Combine them well. Shape the beef mix into one inch balls.

Bake for 25 minutes or until the balls are no longer pink and the juices run clear.

In a medium pan, combine peanut butter, soy sauce, preservers, sesame oil, chili-garlic mix and the vinegar. Heat to boiling, stirring often.

Pour peanut butter mixture over the top of the meatballs, top with red peppers and return to oven for 5 minutes.

Serve hot.

Nutrition: Calories: 232 Fat: 12g Saturated Fat: 4g Protein: 19g Total Carbs: 12g Fiber: 1g

CONCLUSION

Thank you for reading this book. American Southern food has become inextricably linked to the South's cultural identity. Whether it's deep-fried chicken or barbecued pork, American Southern cuisine is difficult to resist. Southern American cuisine is known around the world for its rich, tangy, and soulful flavors. We hope you enjoyed this eBook and the recipes contained within it.

Each Southern cuisine recipe represents home cooking; each dish embodies the South's traditions and hospitality. Each page contains a different Southern classic, ranging from basic appetizers to delectable desserts. This recipe book contains everything you need to master Southern cuisine. Southern recipes are well-known and extremely popular, and many people prepare them on a daily basis.

Southern cuisine is an American culinary melting pot of sweet, salty, tangy, and savory flavors. Its origins can be traced back to the diverse cuisines of its early settlers, explaining its delightful blend of Native American, European, African, and Latin flavors. The rich agricultural supply of the southern states, combined with diverse cultural influences, resulted in traditional comfort food, which is still enjoyed in restaurants and homes today. Furthermore, you can now make these favorites in your own kitchen and serve up southern comfort food for the entire family.

I encourage you to try all of the recipes in this book and pick your favorites. The recipes are written in a clear and direct manner to guide you through every step of preparing these delectable meals the way I learned them. Of course, you can change them, but I encourage you to start with the DIRECTIONS: and then tweak them to your liking.

Enjoy the flavors of southern cuisine while nurturing your cooking passion.

If you liked this book please consider leaving a review on Amazon, please!